The Talk

A Young Person's Guide to Life's Big Questions

Shawn Davis

ISBN: 978-1-960913-00-5 (Paperback)
ISBN: 978-1-960913-01-2 (Hardcover)
ISBN: 978-1-960913-02-9 (eBook)

First edition

To Jim Schoenfeldt and Walter Blodgett,
who helped save a young man from himself,
to all the other teachers who had to tolerate me as a student,
and to all the students who had to tolerate me as a teacher.

Table of Contents

A Question

I have a question to ask you, but it is not my question—it belongs to one of my former students—so I must begin with the story of how that question came to be asked in the first place.

One of the first lessons I gave my chemistry classes each year was on scale. The method was simple: I would guide my students through a series of forty images, each magnified ten times from the previous. That was it—that was the lesson. Just forty images, yet they were sufficient to take my students on a journey beginning in a maelstrom of galaxies millions of light-years from Earth and ending in the center of a single atom. Of the forty, only twelve could conceivably have been captured by humans, and only six of those were at a scale that could be appreciated with the naked eye. The rest were hypothetical creations, simulations of a reality none of us could directly observe.

The method was simple, but the effect was profound. Afterward, I would ask my students to write a reflection, and a hush would fall over the room that would last as long as I allowed it to. Eventually, in a tone respectful of the silence I was breaking, I would ask if anyone had thoughts to share. Another long silence would ensue. Finally, one brave student would dare to speak, followed eventually by another, and another, the rest listening and nodding like those attending a funeral, a common weight pressing down upon them all.

During one such discussion a girl confessed, "This lesson terrified me." But why? Why should a simple lesson on scale terrify her? Because she, like most of her classmates, had lived her entire life with the delusion that her world had been transcended and transformed by human ingenuity into something rather tame and manageable and that her life and actions were matters of great import to that world. Now, in the span of a class period, she had learned that the world she knew was only an infinitesimal fraction of the world that exists, that the objective reality around her was incomprehensibly vast and unimaginably powerful, that the only thing keeping her and the rest of us from complete annihilation was our near total isolation. The blue sky above her head belied the endless sea of blackness beyond it. Not only was she utterly insignificant; she was also utterly alone. Her classmates, too, felt that terror. They all shared her loneliness. They were all undone. The funeral they were attending was their own.

How do you begin to address that feeling of insignificance and isolation? By asking the right question, the question another young lady dared to ask when it was her turn to speak. She simply said, "This lesson made me wonder: Why bother doing anything?"

Why bother doing anything? What a question! That question is *the* question, the question of all questions, the most important question any young person could ask, the most important question *anyone* could ask. *Why bother doing anything?* Indeed! In the context of eternity and infinitude, what significance could our puny lives possibly have? What should we do with this speck of time we have on this speck of dust floating in the vast cosmic darkness? Does it even matter? That question is life's fundamental question, the question whose answer ought to guide our every attitude and action but which we instead often fill our lives with distractions to avoid. But why? Why should we avoid it? Because it is so utterly terrifying! The question fills us with dread, not only because we fear the answer but because we fear *there is no answer.*

It is a rare and wonderful thing to be in a room full of teenagers completely undone, and I always resisted the urge to swoop in to save them. Instead, I would let them walk out that day with that dread question lingering over their heads, not because I enjoyed watching them stagger under the weight of it but in the interest of timing. The school year, after all, had only just begun, and I had only just met them. It would take time to earn the respect and trust I would need to help them with such a burden. Besides, time spent under a burden is often time well spent.

I confess I did not always help as much as I might have. I suppose I hid behind the noble-sounding notion that it would be wrong for me to impose my own answers on a captive audience of impressionable teenagers. Besides, wasn't the way I went about my business each day lesson enough for those paying attention? Perhaps. But unspoken lessons are easily missed or misunderstood, and as the years passed, I felt a growing burden of my own, the burden of the ineffectual. Year after year,

I weighed my students down with hard questions and then let them slip out my door without ever giving them the tools they needed to answer them. Eventually, I came to realize that help unoffered is its own imposition.

One year I finally decided to do something about it. For one day, I would set aside my curriculum and speak the unspoken; I would not only ask life's big questions but dare to suggest how my students might go about seeking their answers. That lesson would come to be known as *The Talk*. At first it was short, just a few of my personal reflections about life, but over the years it grew until I could no longer get through all I wanted to say. Students would ask me about it months in advance and remind me about it years later. It came to represent my best reasons for having become a teacher in the first place, a lesson worthy of my speck of time on this speck of dust.

But why should my students listen to anything I had to say? Because I was honest with them; because day after day I told them the truth as I saw it, without apology, and attempted to live such that my words matched my life and my life matched my words. After all, only a fool trusts a hypocrite.

And only a fool trusts a stranger. That makes this book tricky to write. You are not one of my students. I have not earned your trust and respect. You do not know me. I am a stranger, and for all you know, I may be a hypocrite as well. Or, I may be a fool and not know what I'm talking about. My only hope is that truth and sincerity have a recognizable ring to them, just as falsehood and guile do, and that my words themselves reveal me for who and what I am. That is the risk I must take.

Still, clever people use words as an artifice to twist the truth, and perhaps I am one of those people. So, don't trust me. Question everything I have to say. When what you read rings true, resist accepting it. Put it through the most rigorous testing you can muster and embrace it only if it passes every test, and even then only tentatively. When what you read rings false, resist dismissing it. Wrestle with it in all humility, considering the possibility that the truth is obscured from you by your own false preconceptions and biases. It is only when you can admit you may be wrong and are willing to grapple with uncomfortable ideas that you stand to grow. That is the risk you must take.

There is no cheating life's big questions. You cannot avoid them, and no one can answer them for you. This book is not an answer key but a guide, a tool to help you begin to answer life's big questions *for yourself*. To get anywhere in the endeavor will require effort on your part, and not a little. Each chapter contains challenges, and it is up to you to personalize them, to zero them in on your life, to see them as worthy adversaries and grapple with them with all your might. You have no choice, really. Life demands your response. It demands your action. That is why the questions are unavoidable, because inaction is not an option. You may not simply admire the questions from a distance or even admire your answers to them. You must *act* in the direction of your answers, because your actions prove your answers. In that sense, it doesn't even matter what you *say* your answers are; what matters is what you *do*. So, as you read, don't just read. Act.

While in my heart I will always be a teacher, I write as I leave the teaching profession behind. The mirror reminds me each day that I have already given, for better or for worse, many of the sweetest years of my life to my students. Most are now grown up and no longer have need of me, which was precisely the point in having taught them in the first place. I write this, then, not for them but for a generation I will never have the privilege to teach, for those who brim with future and promise even as my beard grays and my scalp thins. My hope is that I write it... for you.

I, too, once brimmed with future and promise. But the future has plodded into the present, and the present into the past. Promise has given way to reality, and reality to history. Gone is the young man with unlimited potential; each day brings nearer instead a man too old to do much of anything for anyone. Behind me, memories crash in ever-growing waves as my legs tremble in the surf. Before me stretch cliffs I have yet to scale. I do not know how I will climb them, but I do know I cannot stay here, so I look for the next slippery handhold and pull. It is from this posture that I write, in gratitude, sadness, and hope. The older I get, the less certain I become of some things, the more certain I become of others, and the more I weep.

With that, I humbly present to you... *The Talk.*

Greatness

I was raised by excellent parents. They gave me enough freedom to make decisions for myself and enough guidance that they could generally trust me with that freedom. School came easily to me. I was a smart kid who got good grades.

At the age of twelve, though, I began to flounder. I was insecure and didn't know who I was or how to navigate a world of ever-increasing change. I found it preferable to bully rather than be bullied, so that's what I did. I also had a mouth that got me into trouble. I got involved with some kids who weren't the best influences on me, and if I'm being perfectly honest, I wasn't the best influence on them, either. It wasn't long before I was in danger of failing the sixth grade.

One of my uncles happened to visit around that time, and, presumably at my mother's request, sat me down for a little talk. Armed with my latest report card, he went on the attack: "So, let me get this straight: You have an 'F' in Social Studies, a 'D' in English, a 'D' in Math, and a 'C' in Science?" I said, "A 'C' is average." My uncle just stared at me, and suddenly I felt very small. He was a man I deeply respected, a man who had emigrated to the United States as a boy about my age, learned a new language, and built himself into a successful businessman. Finally, he spoke, and I'll never forget what he said to me: "*Average? Is that what you want to be?*"

I don't know how I replied. I was not an easy young man to talk to. But here I am, thirty-five years removed from that conversation, and his words still haunt me. *Average? Is that what I want to be?*

Please don't misunderstand me—being average is nothing to be ashamed of. We will all be average in some things, above average in others, and below average in still others. But to *aspire* to be average is another thing entirely, particularly with all the opportunity and potential I had. Aspiring to be average was pathetic, and I knew it.

Even so, things didn't turn around for me just then. Sometimes life's most important moments begin with the casting of a seed, a small, uncertain act whose full significance becomes apparent only much later.

My parents, realizing the public school system was content to let me quietly fail, made the necessary arrangements and sacrifices to send me to a small, rural private school. I didn't like my new school much at first. The rules were strict and, as I said, I had a mouth that got me into trouble. Perhaps that's why, in my own teaching career, I have always had a soft spot for mouthy slackers. At that school, though, I found something I sorely lacked and desperately needed.

My public-school teachers had always been nice enough, but that was the problem: They too readily accepted me for who I was. The teachers at my new school were different. They made half the money of my public-school teachers and had sacrificed more lucrative careers to teach *me*. Why would they do that? It certainly wasn't to accept me for who I was. No, they did it because they saw in me the person I could become, and they fully expected me to become *that* version of myself. They showed me respect by refusing to share in my low expectations. They saw it as their primary duty to teach me not English or Math but what it meant to be a *man*, a man worthy of the title and prepared to take on other titles in time, titles like *husband* and *father*. They did the greatest thing an adult can do for a young person: They expected greatness of me.

At first, I resisted these new expectations, but in time, a funny thing happened: Their expectations proved prophetic. I, too, began to expect more of myself. Eventually, I even dared to expect greatness.

That's why I became a teacher. At a critical juncture in my life, a few teachers cared enough about me to expect more of me than I expected of myself. I have never thanked them for it, but I have tried to honor their legacy by doing for others what they did for me. Like them, I may never know my full impact, but that knowledge is not what drives a teacher. What drives a teacher is never what lies behind. At the heart of teaching is hope, and hope looks forward. A teacher casts his work into the wind, knowing not where it will be blown, in hopes that a seed will land somewhere it can take root and outlive the one who cast it.

Many years ago, a seed cast by others took root in me. Now, I cast my own seed into the wind.

So, I ask: *Who has expected greatness of you? Do you expect it of yourself?*

Privilege

We each begin life with certain advantages and disadvantages that we have done nothing to deserve. The first thing we are given, life itself, is the privilege of all privileges. Whatever else life brings us, having it at all should fill us with humility and gratitude.

Life owes you nothing. It is a gift given without promises. When you approach it in that way, it will never disappoint you; you will find yourself able to accept every benefit as an unexpected blessing and every difficulty as a necessary cost of existence.

The alternative to a posture of humble gratitude is one of entitlement, which produces thanklessness toward your own blessings and envy toward the blessings of others. Adopting a mindset of entitlement quashes any chance you have of feeling fulfilled by life, because it resigns you to being forever preoccupied by what you do not have. It causes your tolerance for difficulties to shrink until you have little tolerance for them at all. It encourages you to see life's obstacles as injustices, to become preoccupied with silly notions of fairness, as if the world owed you something.

"It's not fair!" is the mantra not of the poor and oppressed but of the rich and spoiled. My brother grew so tired of hearing his teenage daughters use the phrase that one day, when his daughters told him something wasn't fair, he said, "You know what? You're right. It isn't fair. In fact, your life is full of unfairness. Let's list some of the ways: First, you've been born into a loving family with two parents; lots of kids don't have that. You get to live in a nice house in a nice neighborhood with safe streets; lots of kids don't have that, either. You get to go to a school where you have teachers and friends who care about you; lots of kids don't have that. You live in a country that provides you with tremendous freedom and opportunity; lots of kids don't have that. You have plenty to eat, and when you're sick, you receive the best possible medical care; lots of kids don't have those things, either. So, when you say, 'It's not fair,' you are absolutely right. Life has been very unfair to you. It's just that, in your case, in virtually every way, it has been unfair *in your favor*."

If you are a typical American youth, you are one of the most privileged people to have ever lived. Virtually everything you have has been bought and paid for by others. While children in other parts of the world die as infants, live with perpetual disease, or work long hours doing dangerous, menial work so their families can eat a few meals a week, you get to invest in yourself for at least eighteen years while someone else provides for your basic needs. The poor and oppressed of the world don't pout, "It's not fair!"—they know the world too well to dare. But when life is perpetually unfair in your favor, it is tempting to believe that you deserve it.

If you don't feel privileged, it's likely you've fallen into playing the comparison game, measuring what you have against what those around you have. There are no winners in this game. There is always someone who has been given more than you, someone with gifts and blessings to wish were yours. Perhaps you even found yourself saying as you read my brother's little rant, "Well, *I* don't have a loving family, or a nice house, or a good school..." It is all too easy to slip into that mindset. Instead, take your focus off what others have and consider the ways in which you have been blessed. Even without knowing you, I can list a few. First, you possess this book. While you may not think that a great privilege, consider what it means: You had enough disposable income to buy it, had someone care enough about you to get it for you, had access to a library, or had a bookstore near enough to steal it from. Any one of those is a great privilege. Second, you can obviously read, also a great privilege.

Is that the full extent of your privilege? I doubt it. But I don't know you, so I don't know all the ways in which you've been blessed.

So, I ask: *In what ways have you been blessed?*

Perhaps you need more context. While the comparison game is insidious, it can be instructive to play it with a broader perspective. We tend to think of our own lifestyle as *normal*, the lifestyles of those poorer than we are as *impoverished*, and the lifestyles of those wealthier than we are as *extravagant*. But if we compare the American median income—about $60,000 per year—with the world median income—about $10,000 per year—we find that, compared to the rest of the world, our *entire nation* lives extravagantly. We live in giant homes. We hoard and waste huge stockpiles of material goods. We eat far more food than we need. We use many times our fair share of energy. Are we not privileged? Yes, we are—deeply so. It's just that, when everyone we know is a king or a queen, it is easy not to notice each other's crowns, except when it benefits our self-pity or vanity to compare them.

Have you ever lived in a war zone? Have you ever spent the night wondering if the next bomb will take more than your eardrums and the following morning sifting through rubble to find what's left of your family and neighbors? Have you ever had a raiding party sweep through your village killing, raping, and burning everything in its path? How many children do you know who have lost body parts to land mines? The last war on American soil was the Civil War, a war of our nation's own devising, and we are now many generations removed from it. We still participate in wars today, but at a comfortable distance. We send highly equipped professionals and machines to do our fighting for us, not to protect our *lives* but our *interests*, while the rest of us stroke our patriotic egos with high talk of *rights* and *liberty*.

Were you born into slavery? Has your every action been dictated by others, not for your benefit but for theirs? No, you and I enjoy a measure of freedom few have ever known, and it was not our blood that purchased it. Our freedom is not a right we have won but a privilege conferred on us by those who sacrificed much that we might have it.

I may not know you personally, but if you have grown up in America, then I do know this: You are deeply blessed. You are a rich kid at your birthday party every single day. You could spend your time complaining that somewhere there is a slightly richer kid getting a slightly nicer party, or you could accept your blessings with humble gratitude.

You are granted opportunity, through no effort of your own and that you therefore do not deserve, that has been granted to only a tiny fraction of those who have ever lived. Even the poorest of us are far

more fortunate than the vast majority of others in the world. If you
don't believe me, take a trip to a third-world country, and while you're
there, visit some of its poorer sections, if you dare. Once you've spent
time in the slums of Liberia, or among the untouchables of India, or
in a shanty town in Mexico, or on the fields of genocide in South
Sudan, or in an e-waste dump in China, or in an AIDS-ravaged village
in Swaziland, or on the barren hillsides of Haiti, or in a sweatshop in
Bangladesh, or in any of the innumerable other such places in the
world, you will never again complain about someone else's privilege
without having your words catch in your throat. There are people
around the world who would risk their lives, who are *currently risking
their lives*, for a tiny fraction of the opportunity you have obtained
simply by virtue of having been born *here* and not *there*.

You have been given a precious gift. Do not squander it.

So, I ask: *What are you doing with the opportunity you've been given?*

Victimhood

It is impossible to talk about privilege without also talking about victimhood. A lot of terrible things happen to a lot of people. People are victimized by abuse, discrimination, poverty, addiction, war, disease, natural disasters, and just plain bad luck. The types and degrees of victimization differ, but we have all been victimized by something at some point, because victimization is a natural consequence of existence. Sometimes people are victimized by forces outside their control; sometimes they victimize themselves. Regardless, once we've been victimized, none of us can choose not to have been victimized; we can only choose how to respond.

Never indulge your victimization by labeling yourself a victim, regardless of how much you deserve the title. Labels have a way of stigmatizing you, of becoming permanent parts of your identity. The victim label is particularly demeaning and damning, because the label itself implies weakness and helplessness. What's worse, it doesn't stop with you. When you label yourself a victim, you compel those around you to pay homage to your victimhood. Don't do that. Remember, we've all suffered victimization in one way or another; no good comes from glorifying it.

The only one who can give final assent to your victimhood is you. You always have a choice: You can allow victimization to consume you, or you can consume it. To merely survive it is not an option, because to survive it is to let it consume you still, only bite by bite rather than all at once, to let it loiter in your life and chew at you forever. The only way to truly overcome victimization is to *transcend* it, to realize a level of potential made possible only by having gone through it. When you transcend your victimization, you don't just survive—you *win*. *It* no longer eats *you*; *you* eat *it*. You *redeem* your suffering; you turn it from an evil into a good.

How do you do that? By climbing. Victimization places obstacles before you, some small, others mountains with sheer rock faces and no footholds, and dares you to climb. Perhaps you are no rock climber, but faced with a big enough rock, you will have to become one. As you begin that process, don't be ashamed to ask a more experienced climber to lend you the tools and teach you to use them, and don't be discouraged if at first you feel weak and heavy. Never let go, and never rush. Learn to embrace the pain that comes with the climb. Pain affirms your mortality and trains you in humility; it forces you to depend on others and spurs you to grow. Be grateful for pain. Don't ignore it or deny it. Don't anesthetize yourself from it. Swallow it and make it a part of you. Mine it for the lessons it can teach you. That is how you transcend victimization, by climbing its obstacles and consuming its pain. There is no way around it; there is only over and through.

And once you've climbed that first rock? Well, then you'll be a rock climber, something only those who have climbed rock can claim. How will you know when you've reached that point? When you are grateful for your suffering; when contemplating it fills you with strength rather than weakness; when you see your loss as gain. Not that you would necessarily choose to go through it again or wish it upon others, but only once you can truthfully say you are grateful for your victimization have you transcended it. And then? Then you are free to look around, to behold a new world, or rather an old world made new. As you do, you will notice others who have the same rock to climb and would welcome a helping hand, not from just anyone but from someone who *knows*, from someone like *you*.

So, I ask: *Are you a victim or a transcender? What are you prepared to do about it?*

Admittedly, I have to this point avoided an obvious connection between privilege and victimhood: There are those who have obtained their privilege *by* victimizing others. In such cases, it is easy for the victim to have an insatiable hunger for justice, but that's just the problem—the desire is insatiable. There are many injustices that will simply never be made right, and to expect otherwise is to set yourself up to be consumed by frustration. Injustice, like pain, is a birthright we all receive with admission into this life: a firm, inescapable reality. Justice, by contrast, is a fickle mistress, alluring but elusive, ever delivering less than she promises. Spend your life chasing her and only one thing is certain: You will have spent your life.

There are also those who enjoy privilege passed down to them by ancestors who victimized others to obtain it. But if rectifying the injustices of the present is intractable, rectifying the injustices of the past is absurd. The only way to do it is to hold accountable those who have done nothing wrong—a peculiar form of justice, indeed. Besides, every one of us has a family tree littered with rapists and murderers, oppressors and thieves; we would all do well to approach the injustices of the past with a measure of humility.

Not that any of us particularly love justice anyway. We seek it only when we wish to claim what we believe to be rightfully ours, never to take from ourselves to give to others. The average American makes six times the global average. Is that because we are six times more *deserving*? Is the disparity *just*, or does it arise at least in part from our willingness to exploit others with our military and economic might? If you think it at all unjust, there is a simple way to prove it: Give away what you have until you have only what you *deserve*. Funny thing is, if everyone did that, things would be exactly the way they are. We all already have that opportunity, and we keep what we keep. And if we do give away some of what we have to others? Is it out of what we believe to be rightfully *theirs* or *ours*? As a duty to *justice* or an act of *generosity*? With a sense of *contrition* or *magnanimity*? It is not only our actions that reveal us for who we are but our attitudes as well. None of us too much mind injustice so long as it is in our favor.

What we are actually saying when we lament injustice is not that we love justice but that *this particular injustice* is one *we don't like*. But why should we expect a world full of things we like? To even desire such a world is to desire injustice, because getting things our way means others don't get them theirs. And who are we to tell the world what it ought to provide us, anyway? To expect a hospitable world is hubris. Instead, expect the opposite. Expect a world that may destroy you at its whim at any moment. You live because every ancestor you've ever had has persevered, not because the world has made it easy for them. Let their perseverance inspire you to persevere as well, not in a world full of justice but in a world full of reality.

If the world truly owes you nothing, then it also does not owe you justice. This fact, so plain to lion and gazelle, is sometimes lost on primates who wear fancy clothes and live in fancy dwellings. Neither lion nor gazelle question whether it is *just* for the lion to catch and eat the gazelle or *just* for the gazelle to get away and let the lion starve. Justice is the delusion of the self-entitled. To desire it is to desire a world that is not this world.

That said, the world does mete out its own brand of justice, holding us accountable not only for our own actions but for the actions of our ancestors. Theirs, after all, are the impulses that course through our minds and the blood that pumps through our veins. We are the products of not only the most successful farmers, doctors, and war heroes in our families but also the most successful murderers, thieves, and cowards. All of that is in us; all of it makes us who we are. That realization should fill us with humility, but not only with humility. Strange as it may sound, it should also fill us with gratitude. Consider how tenuous is the line of your ancestry, how many people had to mate in just the right combinations at just the right moments to pass on just the right genetic material to eventually form *you*. You can't be too upset that one of your many great-great-great-grandparents was conceived when one of your great-great-great-great-grandfathers raped one of your great-great-great-great-grandmothers, can you? After all, without that atrocity and innumerable others, you could not even exist.

The same argument applies, by the way, not just to your *own* ancestors but to *everyone's*. Had *any* of them acted any differently, you would not exist. If you are an American of African descent, it is likely that your ancestors were the slaves of the ancestors of some of the people around you. It's also likely that, as a result of the exploitation and abuse of your ancestors by theirs, they have a more privileged starting point in life than you do: They grow up in nicer houses, go to nicer schools, receive better medical care, and so on. But you *exist*, don't you? Think about it: If any of their ancestors or your ancestors had acted any differently at any point in time leading up to the moment of your conception, you would not even be here to contemplate the injustice! Altering even one act of oppression in the distant past would erase you from existence. Had the Inquisition and the Holocaust not occurred, no one born after those events would exist. Had European settlers not displaced Native Americans from their land, whether you are descended from those European settlers, those Native Americans, or some combination of the two, you would not exist. Now, you could certainly contend that *the* world might be a better place had those events not occurred, but you could not contend that *your* world would be better, because *your* world would not exist. The world you have inherited is the only one you could have inherited. You may be appalled by it, but you must be gratefully appalled.

You may think this line of argumentation escapist, a bit of logical sleight of hand designed to draw your attention away from the real issue, but it's not. It puts your apprehension of your place in this world precisely where it ought to be, on the incredible unlikelihood of your having a place in it at all. Whatever your world is, *you are alive*, and an incomprehensible number of things had to happen just the way they did for that to be the case. Your life has come at the expense of a nearly infinite number of other potential lives that will now never get to be lived because *you* get to live. For that, you should be very, very grateful.

As for injustices perpetrated against you directly, here again, look to the past. You would not likely find your ancestors impressed by what you suffer. I say this not to shame you but to encourage you. Those broken by suffering do not leave descendants; those who persevere and overcome do, and that is what every one of your ancestors has done. The product of their perseverance? The proof of their triumph? *You*. Your very existence testifies to your pedigree and potential. You are descended from the triumphant, from those who have endowed you with what you need to triumph as well.

There will always be injustice, and there will always be those who profit from it at the expense of others. To fixate on that is to fail to apprehend life with sufficient gratitude, but it is also much worse: It is to fail to apprehend life's very meaning and purpose. You have but one life. You could spend it taking stock of what others have and resenting it, or you could spend it taking stock of what *you* have and *doing something with it*. You have been victimized? Granted. What are you going to do with your life? You are privileged? Granted. What are you going to do with your life? Categorizing yourself by either your victimization or your privilege fails to give any clarity to life's fundamental question: *What are you going to do with it?*

Wallowing in victimhood only demeans and paralyzes you. Don't do it. Redeem it instead. Transcend it instead.

So, I ask: *You have but one life to live. What are you going to do with it?*

Suffering

The ugly cousin of "It's not fair" is "Why me?" Unlike "It's not fair," which we say when life doesn't give us what we believe we deserve, we ask, "Why me?" when it gives us what we believe we don't deserve and can't understand—when we are made to suffer and don't know why. When we ask, "Why me?", what we really want to know is, "Is there a *reason* for my suffering? Is there a *purpose* to my suffering?" A woman in labor never asks, "Why me?" because she knows both the cause of her suffering and its effect, and that sense of reason and purpose gives her the capacity to endure it.

"Why me?", like "It's not fair," conceals an insidious bias. Which of us asks, "Why me?" when in a lifetime of driving on busy roads we have never been in a serious accident? Which of us asks, "Why me?" when we get a paycheck for relatively easy work that puts us in the top 10%, or 1%, or 0.1% of people on the planet? Which of us asks, "Why me?" when we go to the grocery store and find the shelves brimming with inexpensive food? Which of us asks, "Why me?" when a highly technical surgery is conducted on our behalf, or when a life-threatening condition is averted by our simply taking a pill, or when corrective lenses are prescribed that enable us to see, or when the women and babies in our families routinely survive childbirth? The problem is not that we have no legitimate reasons for asking, "Why me?"; the problem is that we tend only to ask it when *un*fortunate things happen to us. This tendency reveals a posture of self-absorbed entitlement. *Why me?* Indeed, why *me?* What right do *I* have to the blessings I've received? None. They are not a right—they are a gift.

There was a well-respected woman in a church I once attended, a loving mother and friend, the sort of person who routinely put others' lives before her own. One day she was traveling down the highway and saw another motorist stranded on the side of the road.

She pulled up behind the other car, found out what the other motorist needed, and walked to the trunk of her own car to get it. They were the last steps she would ever take. As she leaned over her trunk, another car veered off the road and smashed into her legs, ripping them in half.

How shocking it was! Just the week before, I had seen the woman in church, walking with unsuspecting ease, both of us taking our legs for granted. A few weeks later, I would see her again, with stubs that failed to reach the edge of her wheelchair, she and everyone around her suddenly keenly aware of her legs and theirs. If ever anyone had a right to ask, "Why me?", it was she.

The first time I saw her after the accident, I strained to focus on her face as she was wheeled past. I attempted to affect a kind, nonchalant air, as if nothing were wrong or different, as if I hadn't even noticed that she now had no legs. But she saw through my awkward act, and what did she do as our eyes met? She smiled at me! And what a smile! It was a smile that said, "It's okay. You needn't pretend not to notice my legs. I've lost them, and it's okay." Perhaps it was a new smile, the sort of smile given by special dispensation to those who have lost much with uncommon grace, or perhaps it was the same smile she had possessed all along, made more brilliant now only in contrast to its gruesome new context. Whatever the case, in this once-common woman now shone a magnificence of character that made me gasp.

"Why me?" Why *not* me? What makes me more deserving of legs than she? Nothing. But am I more fortunate? It is true that I have legs and she does not. But my character is theoretical; hers has been tested by fire. Perhaps her legless existence is more meaningful than my legged existence will ever be. Perhaps her legless existence is more meaningful than her own legged existence could ever have been. Is that possible? Could that really be? I'm sure not a day goes by that she does not miss her legs, but is her life now worse or better for having gone through the tragedy? It has certainly made her life more significant to *me*; would she say that it is now more significant to *her*? If she had it to do over again, would she have stopped to help her fellow motorist that day? Could she have even changed that single act without changing everything about who she was, or would passing by another in need that one time have made her the *sort* of person who passes by others in need?

It has been many years since I've forgotten that woman's name, and I used to feel guilty for having forgotten it. If anyone's name warranted remembering, it was hers. But I came to realize that what I most needed to remember was not her name but her smile. Imagine living your life so indelibly that others remember your smile long after they've forgotten your name!

We can allow life's tragedies to make us bitter and resentful, or we can see them as tests of our character and humility, allowing them to make us ever thankful, not only for *a* life but for *this very life*—for *my* life and *your* life. Each of us has only one life, unique from every other, and we all have reason to ask, "Why me?", not in bitterness or despair but in awe and gratitude.

So, I ask: *Why you?*

Goals

Goals matter. Without them, you're likely to waste a lot of time aimlessly drifting through life, and time is not something you have in abundance.

A goal is not the same thing as a wish. A goal is something you work toward; a wish is something you hope will happen to you. Not sure if what you have is a wish or a goal? It's easy to tell. All you have to do is ask yourself a follow-up question: What am I doing to make it a reality? If your answer is, "Not much," then what you have is a wish, not a goal.

Not all goals matter equally. It takes wisdom to discern which are good goals, and wisdom is hard to come by when you're young because you have so little experience to draw from. Without wisdom, every decision you make is made foolishly, so you may be wise to make attaining wisdom your first goal—and your first act of wisdom. Wisdom is found in nature only by mining a lot of rock. Only once you've blistered your hands and sweated through your shirt will you find it on your own, and that wisdom, the wisdom mined with your own hammer and pick, is that which you will most treasure. There is, however, an easier way. Those who have mined a lot of rock are wise enough to know that they cannot take what they've found to their graves, and they are often eager to share it with those humble enough to ask. That may be your second act of wisdom: to ask someone for some of theirs. Having done that, you set yourself up for your third act of wisdom: to shut up and listen.

So, I ask: *How much digging, asking, and listening have you done?*

As you grow and mature, so too will your goals. As an ambitious young man, I had goals of becoming a professional athlete, a revolutionary musician, a celebrated artist, and a brilliant scientist, and I was prepared to measure my success and failure in those terms. There was nothing wrong with any of those goals, each of which came from a sincere desire to do something great, except that they were all about *me*. And why shouldn't they have been? I was a young man eager to make my way and my mark in the world. My way. My mark.

I am no longer a young man. I am nearly fifty. I have long since given up the goals of my youth. It is not that I abandoned them in despair after failing to achieve them, though I have certainly failed often enough. No, what discouraged me most from the goals of my youth were not my failures but my successes, that they proved so hollow. It was my successes that taught me to aspire to better goals, goals I would be proud to achieve and ashamed not to. Goals that mattered more had to matter more to me.

Now I define my success and failure by the honest answers to three questions I ask myself every day:

Am I a good husband?

Am I a good father?

Do I do my job well?

Goals like these are hard to achieve. I've been married for twenty years. Do you think you go through twenty years of marriage on loving feelings? No, it's a grind. Marriage is a daily, moment-by-moment exposition of my most selfish attitudes and deepest flaws. It relentlessly demands that I lay aside my own good for the good of another just as selfish as I am. That is hard to do. But it is also good. It is very good.

Do you have any idea how hard it is to be a good father, to be everything your children need you to be—dependable and honest and patient and firm and productive and available and giving and kind—all at the same time, every day? Again, it's a grind. But it is also good. It is very good.

Compared with the other two, doing my job well is easy enough, but in the workplace there are still pressures to compromise personal integrity at every turn. Opportunities abound to gossip and shirk and complain and lie. Navigating that minefield every day is not easy. It's a grind. But it is also good. It is very good.

I don't achieve these goals as often as I'd like. There are times I end the day staring at my bedroom ceiling, saying to myself, "Man, what a lousy husband I was today," or "Man, what a lousy father I was today," or "Man, what a lousy job I did today." Life is a grind. To accomplish these goals all day, every day—day in, day out, day in, day out—is difficult in the extreme. But worthy goals are always difficult.

The beauty of goals like being a good spouse or parent or worker is that they are accessible to all. You don't have to be particularly athletic or good-looking or smart or creative or rich or talented to be a good husband or wife, a good father or mother, or a good worker. What a great comfort that is, because few of us are remarkable in any of those ways.

As for the goals of my youth? Had I achieved them to a greater degree, I may have made it all the harder to achieve worthier goals. How many wealthy, famous people lament the toll their wealth and fame have taken on those closest to them? How many successful men have traded their wives and children for the accolades and affections of strangers? If my family is the price of my success, then I am grateful to have had so little of it.

When a goal takes prominence in your life, it requires the sacrifice of other goals, the sacrifice of yourself. Goals are, by definition, linked to sacrifices. A goal is a focus, and one cannot have a focus without excluding that which is outside that focus. A sacrifice is an exchange, and one cannot make an exchange without giving something up. Indeed, your life is one giant, continuous sacrifice being poured out on the altar of your choosing, moment by moment and day by day. It is spent relentlessly whether you intend to spend it or not. If you have an hour of time in the evening and use it to get ice cream, you are sacrificing everything else you might have done with that hour to get ice cream. If you use that hour instead to write a poem, or play a game, or watch a sunset, or make love, or fix your bicycle, then you are sacrificing everything else you might have done with that hour to do that. Whether or not you've been aware of it, you've been sacrificing your life for your entire life, and you will continue to do so until you have no more life left to sacrifice. Your only choice is what you sacrifice it to.

So, I ask: *What is worth so much that you would give up all else for it?*

Identity

Perhaps the most important and terrifying question you have to answer as a young person is, "Who am I?" As you grow into an adult, you must transition from defining yourself in the terms of your parents and other adults to defining yourself in your own terms. You must shed the authority of others and establish authority over yourself. You must free yourself from the vision others have established for you and establish your own vision. This transition may strain your relationships with adults, particularly your parents, but don't shy away from it—it is both natural and essential.

So, who are you? What pressure, to have to define yourself at an age at which you are only just getting to know yourself! It's okay. You don't have to have it all figured out at once; you develop your identity over time. But developing it will require work. So, how do you *begin* to develop it? Fortunately, it is not that hard to do.

One way to define your identity is to lump together your genetic endowment, your actions, and your experience: You are the sum of everything with which you were born, everything you've done, and everything that has happened to you. The problem with this definition is that it is paralyzing. You cannot change the past, so if the past is all that shapes your identity, then there is simply nothing you can do about who you are—you are a prisoner.

Your identity is formed in part by your past, but only in part, and not the most important part. Think of your past as merely a starting point. You are not a rock or a tree or a fish, you are a human being—you don't get to decide that. You were born in a certain place, in a certain community, in a certain body with certain characteristics—you don't get to decide those things, either. Your past may have included things chosen for you or chosen for yourself, but at this point those things are just as immutable as your genetics—you no longer get to control any of them, either. But everything leading up to the present moment merely defines a new starting point: your *now*.

The part of your identity that is uniquely yours to control is what you do next, and that is actually an immense amount to control. Who are you? *You are your aim.* You are a seeker of whatever you seek. If you seek God, you are a God-seeker. If you seek power, you are a power-seeker. If you seek freedom, you are a freedom-seeker. If you seek truth, you are a truth-seeker. If you seek comfort, you are a comfort-seeker. If you seek to serve, you are a service-seeker. If you seek revenge, you are a revenge-seeker. If you seek peace, you are a peace-seeker.

Your aim is not just *what* you train your eye on; it is *how* you train your eye. In that sense, your aim *is* your eye, the very lens through which you see your entire life. Your aim works in both directions, transforming what you see not only from one side of the lens but from the other as well: In one direction, it establishes all you aspire to do and be, and in the other it rots or redeems all you were born or have done or have had done to you. Your future, ethereal as it is, is yet safeguarded by your aim. Does it promise doom or deliverance, want or fulfillment, despair or hope? Your aim decides that. Your past, immutable as it is, is yet the slave of your aim. Does it serve resentment or forgiveness, guilt or redemption, thanklessness or gratitude? Your aim decides that. Your aim has the power to turn every good into an evil or every evil into a good. Through it you interpret your past, give purpose to your present, and cast a vision for your future.

I told you that it is not that hard to figure out who you are. If you answered the question at the end of the last chapter, then you've already begun that process. What is worth so much that you would give up all else for it? *That* is your aim. *That* is your identity. Who are you? You are a seeker of *that*.

So, I ask: *What is your aim? What do you seek?*

What if what you seek is an elusive thing, a vague notion not clear enough or firm enough to guide you in the concrete world of the here and now? How do you give your aim greater focus? I offer three questions to guide you:

Where do you seek to be in five years?

Perhaps you have a ready answer. If so, it likely involves some combination of graduating from high school, succeeding in college, getting a dream job, and meeting the perfect man or woman. Those are nice goals, but they may be just wishes in disguise. Half of college freshmen, for example, will either drop out or graduate only to find themselves unemployed or underemployed. If that many young people fail to achieve even their *five*-year goals, what chance do they have of realizing any goals in the longer term? Why even bother making longer-term goals at all? Stay with me—we'll get there.

Where do you seek to be in twenty-five years?

Twenty-five years! An eternity! In twenty-five years, you will be *my* age, middle-aged. It seems so far off, doesn't it? Let me tell you: It goes by in a flash. You will be my age before you know it, your peak years already behind you. Don't you think you ought to have thought about those years before they've come and gone?

Have you ever actually thought twenty-five years ahead? Do you base any of your day-to-day decisions on a vision that reaches that far into the future? Likely not, if you're anything like I was as a young man, and yet the decisions you make today will affect the entire trajectory of your life. In twenty-five years, if you make it that far, who will you be? You will be whatever you have made your aim for those twenty-five years. If you realize only then that you aimed for the wrong things or never really aimed for much of anything, don't be surprised twenty-five years from now to find in the mirror a wrinkling shell of wasted potential staring blankly back at you as you wonder what happened to all those years. You are never freer to make decisions than you are right now. The further through adulthood you get, the more beholden to responsibilities you become. If you want to take control of the trajectory of your life, do it *now*.

By the time you have been out of high school or college just a few years, most of your closest friends from those places, those whose affirmation was so important to you, whose opinions mattered so much to you, will likely have vanished from your life. Best friends will have become just friends, friends will have become acquaintances, and acquaintances will have been forgotten. That may sound sad, but it's not. It's just a normal part of going through life's seasons. Every time you welcome new people into your life, you must let go of others. This transaction is necessary not only to make room for new people but also to give you room to grow into a new person yourself.

Who will be preeminent in your life twenty-five years from now? Whose affirmation and opinions will matter to you then? Likely people you have not yet met, maybe even people who *do not yet exist*. And yet, once those people enter your life, all your priorities will change in an instant. Your life before their arrival will seem like a dream you are just waking from, a dream you can only vaguely remember, as if it were the life of some other person who lived long ago. When that happens, you will apprehend your aim for all those years with new eyes. Will you apprehend it with gratitude or regret?

Where do you seek to be in a hundred years?

Well, you'll be dead. Consider, though, the question behind the question: Once you are dead and gone, what will remain? What will you have left behind? In a hundred years, will anyone even remember you existed? What will be different because you existed? How will the people you knew and loved remember you? What part of you will live on in them? What will be your legacy?

Legacy is one of the reasons I became a teacher. An architect may leave behind buildings he's designed, an artist her paintings, a musician his music, but when I walked out of my classroom for the last time, I had nothing tangible to show for two decades of work. I left behind an empty room, a room that would be filled the following fall by a teacher and students unknown to me. That may sound sad, but it's not. Eventually, the architect's buildings crumble, the artist's paintings fade, and the musician's music is forgotten. Given enough time, none of us have much to show for our life's work. But as a teacher, I had the opportunity to leave a *living* legacy. Every student who walked out of my classroom took a part of me with them. That part, however small, would change the course of each of their lives, and the lives of those they touched, and so on. Whatever I sacrificed to them ripples outward even as its intensity wanes, echoing long after I am gone and my name is forgotten. That is my legacy. What will be yours?

If your aim is short and you compromise it by the width of an arrow, how far from your target will you have drifted in five years, or twenty-five, or a hundred? You see, the only way to ensure that the arrow flies true is to aim as far into the future as you can. The most pressing question, then, is not the first but the last, the question of legacy. The way you answer *that* question is your aim of all aims. Take dead aim at *that* question, and the answers to more proximal questions will come into sharp focus. Where do you seek to be in five years, or twenty-five, or a hundred? The key is to answer these questions *in reverse*. After all, how could you possibly make plans for the next five years without first establishing where you seek to be in twenty-five? And how could you possibly know where you seek to be in twenty-five years without first establishing what you desire your legacy to be?

Only by making your legacy your aim can you ensure that your essential goals, those that stir from your very *essence*, remain uncorrupted by a million other, lesser goals that constantly vie for your attention. Only by making your legacy your aim can you summon the courage to act with conviction in the moment, whatever that moment may bring. Bring all other aims into alignment with that one aim, and you will have established a clear path for your life. And because you *are* your aim, you will have also found your identity.

When my son was fifteen, I asked him what he wanted his legacy to be. He said, "I want to be someone others recognize as important." What a great aspiration! After all, what's the alternative? To aspire to be *un*important?

But wait. As soon as you decide you want to be someone others recognize as important, you are faced with another question: *Who* do you wish to see you as important? If you wish to leave a legacy, the things you do cannot matter only to you. People who do things that matter only to themselves leave no legacy, because they give no one anything to remember them for. A legacy, by definition, must matter to others, because a legacy is something you leave behind—*you* won't be here anymore to think it's important! A legacy is not how you define your own life; it is how your life is defined by others.

Your legacy, then, is not simply a matter of what you do but a matter of who you do it for. Who would you want to speak at your funeral? Friends from high school? Professional colleagues? Investors you made wealthy? Adoring fans? Adults in your social circle? Your next-door neighbors? Your children and grandchildren? Whose praise matters to you? Whose honor do you seek?

There will be those who have the right to determine your legacy and those to whom you give the privilege. Never confuse the two. Those who have the right are those who, by no decision of their own, are dependent on you for *their* lives. Those to whom you give the privilege are those who associate with you by mutual consent. When I choose between working late to impress my boss, cutting out early to meet up with my drinking buddies, or getting home as fast as I can to coach my son's baseball team, the choice I make determines who I wish to define my legacy. I know who I want to speak at my funeral, and it shapes every decision I make. Do you?

So, I ask: *What do you wish your legacy to be? Who would you have define it?*

Confusion

Confusion: the alternative to identity.

Your identity is a fixed point of reference in a relativistic world, an anchor to lay hold of when life's chaos swirls about you. When the storm rages in the dark night, a voice on the wind will ask, "Who are you?", and the quality and depth of your answer will determine whether you stand firm or flounder.

Perhaps the dark night has already found you. Do you find yourself chronically anxious or depressed? Have you been told that the problem lies without, that there is nothing wrong with you, that it is the world around you that is responsible? Don't believe it; it's not true. The problem lies within. Anxiety and depression are *responses*: *you* produce them. Whatever the external factors, the problem is *your* problem.

Let that revelation give you hope. After all, if your problem is the world's responsibility, then what must change? The world? Good luck waiting for that to happen. The world is simply the world, the only one you could possibly have inherited. It is responsible for neither the problem nor the solution. You are.

And what is your problem? Perhaps you have a crisis of identity. Anxiety comes when you don't know who you are, depression when you believe you know and don't like what you believe. Both are perfectly natural states. They are not diseases to be cured nor evils to be vanquished. They are, rather, manifestations of the *not yet*, the fitful darkness through which you must pass to be born into the light of a new reality. Anxiety and depression are your friends. They tell you there is something undone that must be done, something *you* must do. They demand action.

It is not easy to act in the darkness. It can feel like you breathe in and in and in and never out. It can feel like you're falling. It can feel like you're a foreigner surrounded by signs you can't read and people you can't understand. It can feel like a pounding in your head. It can feel like an impenetrable silence. I know. In case you haven't noticed, I find life both absurd and wonderful. But I haven't always found it wonderful. I have gone through periods of deep anxiety and depression, particularly as a young man struggling to figure out who I was. It took time for me to get through it, and it didn't just happen. Things began to change only as I began to act. I didn't know what to do, so I did *something*, something that seemed worth doing, and I kept doing that until I figured out who I was, or at least who I wanted to be. I didn't know it at the time, but that was a wise thing to do. As some*thing* undone is done, some*one* undone is also done. Who are you? You are a seeker of what you seek, but you are also a doer of what you do. Action need not always follow vision; sometimes you must act to find a vision. When you don't know who you are, do *something*, something that seems worth doing, and keep doing that until you figure out who you are, or at least who you would like to be.

But could you do better than that? Could you act with more intention than that? You could. Before you leap into action, check your footing; evaluate your surroundings; take inventory of your tools and provisions: Start with what you know. You don't begin life drifting in a void; you begin it on the solid ground of a systematic world. You are born with people all around you who have poked around in that world a lot longer than you have, some of whom have been explicitly tasked with making sure you don't get too badly injured before you've learned to take care of yourself. It's okay to rely on these people; just don't rely on them for too much or for too long.

Question much; doubt little. What's the difference? *Questioning* means trying to understand why things are the way they are; *doubting* means disbelieving things are the way they are. You can question everything without necessarily doubting anything. *Questioning* means starting with the things countless others have learned about the world and poking at them to see how they respond to the poking. *Doubting* means starting with nothing, and it is a lousy place to start—you are simply too limited to get very far on your own. Start with what others have learned, and question your way from there. Really, you have no choice. Without others, not only would you fail to find your answers; you would fail to possess even the language with which to form your questions.

Life is amply confusing on its own; don't create confusion where it doesn't exist. You don't get to make the world whatever you wish it to be. You don't get to make yourself whatever you wish to be. You were born a specific person with specific attributes in a specific place and time. You had specific parents who treated you in a specific way. You grew up within a specific family within a specific community within a specific society. All of these factors have contributed to who you are, and you had little to do with any of them. There is no need to doubt it. Question it all you like, poke and prod it all you like, but don't doubt it. That's your reality. Start with that.

Remember that you were born hopelessly dependent on others, a useless lump of whining flesh. Others have created, nurtured, and shaped you. Don't doubt that; it's true. Don't attempt to liberate yourself from that fact with silly notions of absolute freedom. You are likely less free than you think. You are the product of the generations that have spawned you and of the influences that have conditioned you. It doesn't mean that everything put into you is good or right, but it is good enough, and it is all important. Acknowledge and embrace that.

We determine our identities in large part by who we allow to guide us and who we choose to emulate. When it comes to the quality of the adults in our lives, though, some of us are more fortunate than others. If that frustrates you, do two things: First, temper your expectations of adults, and second, seek out worthier ones to be guided by and to emulate.

Many adults are only pretending. They strut around with an air of composure and self-assurance, but the facade only disguises the deep insecurities of an overgrown child. Such people haven't yet figured out who *they* are; how could they possibly help you figure out who *you* are? Then there are those who make no such pretense, who have been beaten down by life and wear their brokenness on the outside. These hobble along in the cold bitterness of victimhood, convincing themselves that life has cheated them rather than persevering through its tragedies to a better way of being.

You may be tempted to scorn such people. Just remember that you have not yet lived much life, that you have not yet faced all the tragedy you will. Being an adult is no easy task, especially when you've never been taught how to do it—or did you assume that the adults around you all received the help *they* needed? Learn to recognize useless guides without getting sanctimonious about it. There are good reasons there are bad adults; be thankful you are ignorant of a great many of them.

How do you recognize adults worth emulating? It's easy. Worthy adults gladly take on responsibility not only for themselves but for others. That's what true adults do and fake adults shrink back from. It is no great accomplishment to take care of yourself—I've known children of ten or twelve who can do that. To become a true adult, you must become more than *in*dependent; you must become depend*able*. You must cheerfully put the needs of others before your own. When you find someone who does that, pay attention.

Even so, don't mindlessly follow anyone. Even the best adults have their flaws, just as even the worst have things they can teach you. Study the adults around you with humility, choosing which of their attributes and behaviors to emulate and which to eschew. It may take the help of others to figure out who you are, but what you choose to make your aim, how you choose to live your life, is something you must ultimately decide for yourself. Remember, you are not truly yourself until you no longer define yourself in others' terms.

Once you get to that point, once you know who you are, you need not fear being misunderstood, or isolated, or bullied. Once you know who you are, you won't care whether others respect you, because *you know who you are.* You will find in yourself the conviction to confront the challenges and adversities of life with tenacious integrity. And once you become a person like that? Others *will* respect you, because you will have become someone undeniably respectable. You can't become that person, though, until you no longer care whether others respect you or not. You must have better reasons than that to be who you are.

Take your time. Be patient with yourself. You don't go from confusion to identity in an afternoon, and how much joy you find in the journey has less to do with where you are at the present moment and more to do with your attitude: your posture, outlook, and direction. With each step you take in the right direction, regardless of where you begin or where you find yourself along the way, you will be encouraged to take the next step, and the next, and before long you'll find yourself in a new place, a different place, a better place.

Once in that place, take the time to look around, to breathe deeply and take in the fresh air. From there, you'll be able to look back on the ground you've trod and apprehend the obstacles you've overcome not with regret but with gratitude, because everything in your past will have become an indispensable part of who you are. You will find you are exactly where you ought to be. You will be in no rush to move on, nor will you linger too long. You'll stay exactly as long as you should, and then you'll move on to another new place, the next right place.

So, I ask: *Do you live in a state of identity or confusion? What are you prepared to do about it?*

Risk

Life is a risk. Life is also punctuated by moments of great risk, and your identity and legacy are shaped by how you respond in those critical moments. Some examples:

- Whether to take an unpopular stand or to shrink back
- Whether to go to college and what to study
- Whether or when to try tobacco, alcohol, drugs, gambling, sex, pornography, or anything else that's potentially dangerous or addicting
- Whether to interview or audition for something difficult
- Whether to quit your job and start something new
- Whether to ask out a girl or boy you have a crush on
- Whether this is the person you wish to be the mother or father of your children
- Whether to raise your children this way or that
- Whether to flirt with someone who is not your spouse
- Whether to reconcile with or divorce your spouse
- Whether or when to buy your first home, or save for your children's future, or make any other large financial investment
- Whether to go into debt to buy something you want
- Whether to risk your own life to save another's

People often shrink back from moments of great risk, but make no mistake: You cannot avoid them. Decisions will be made one way or the other, whether you are prepared for them or not, whether you make them yourself or allow them to be made for you. Will you face life's great risks with whimsy or conviction? These decisions will shape the course of your life! Get prepared!

The ill-prepared often fail to recognize moments of great risk when they arrive and make decisions based on what is expedient in the moment. Did the drug addict take his first hit because he really wanted to or because he was too weak to withstand peer pressure? Did the pregnant teenager really make love to that boy, or did she just hope to win his affections by yielding to his advances? Did the dropout really believe he was prepared for college, or was he only trying to live up to his father's expectations? Did the debt-ridden housewife really need those things she charged to her secret credit cards, or was she just hoping they would fill the gaping hole in her self-esteem? Failing to recognize moments of great risk is like dancing in the dark. You may be on solid ground, or you may be twirling at the verge of a precipice—you don't know.

There was a boy in a youth group I once led who was affable and funny; everyone liked him. His ebullient personality, however, masked deep insecurities, and he desperately sought the approval of others. When he went to college, he pledged a fraternity, and at one of its parties he drank himself unconscious. That night, in a house full of people, he quietly choked to death on his own vomit. I'm sure that earlier in the evening he had been affable and funny; I'm sure everyone had liked him. All evening long a moment of great risk was staring him in the face, and he failed to recognize it. His very life was hanging on each decision he made, and he didn't know it. How many decisions would he have made differently, had he only known!

I was tasked with calling his closest friends with the news. Those were the hardest phone calls I've ever had to make. I was broken that day. I had had years of opportunities to help prepare that young man for moments of great risk, and I had failed. But any regret I felt paled in comparison to that which I saw etched on the face of his father a few days later at the funeral home. What grief belonged to that man! What grief belongs to him still today, twenty-two years later! Your moments of great risk are not yours alone. The decisions you make in those moments are of great import to a great many people—people of great import to you—and what you do in those moments will reverberate in their lives as well as your own.

Preparing for moments of great risk is one thing, but how do you summon the courage to respond with conviction when those moments come? It's pretty simple, really. If you have taken proper aim, then you will know who you are, and if you know who you are, then you will know what you must do. Courage is simply the commitment to do the right thing even when it is difficult. What do you do in moments of great risk? You do the right thing. And if you can't do everything you wish you could do? You do the best you can under the circumstances and accept the consequences of your actions with grace. That's it.

If you approach moments of great risk with preparedness and courage, then regardless of whether your actions bring reward or punishment, you will find yourself able not only to tolerate the consequences but to embrace them. The leering glances of your naysayers will wilt before the glow of your honor and integrity, and instead of a life tyrannized by guilt, shame, and regret, you will be free to live the winsome life.

So, I ask: *How well prepared are you for moments of great risk?*

You are not special. Thinking ourselves special is the great hubris of humankind, a natural consequence of our self-awareness and will to survive. We each think of ourselves as the most important person in the world, because to us we are. This sense of self-importance helps keep us alive, but it also threatens to make us all little tyrants of our own little worlds. Objectively speaking, few of us are special, and even if we are, we have ample deficiencies to compensate. So, if you don't want to end up a little tyrant of a little world, remind yourself often: "I am not special."

You are not special, but you are unique. No one else can be exactly who you can be, and no one else can do exactly what you can do. Your role in this big world may be a small one, but to those in your little sphere of influence your value may be incalculable. I may not matter much to the world as a whole, but to my wife and children I am one of the most important people in the world. I am less important to my extended family and close friends, still less to my coworkers and casual acquaintances, and of no importance at all to a great many others. Apprehending yourself properly means coming to terms with both your insignificance and significance. An honest life starts with an honest assessment of self. You are neither worthless nor preeminent but somewhere in between.

You are not entitled to success, nor can you inherit failure. Just because your mother is a renowned brain surgeon does not entitle you to her success. Just because your father is an abusive alcoholic does not consign you to his failure. You may benefit from the successes of others or suffer from their failures, but do not confuse those benefits or sufferings with success or failure themselves. Success and failure are derived not from anything you *possess* but rather by the things you *do*. *Your* successes and failures rest on *your* actions and *your* actions alone.

The reason you cannot inherit success or failure is that both require risk, and no one else can take your risks for you. Anything acquired without risk is not earned but given, and being given things never made anyone a success or failure. Wealth or influence or poverty or powerlessness conferred as a birthright are nothing to be either proud or ashamed of. You can claim with pride or shame only those things which you have done yourself, at your own risk. All else is merely circumstance.

There is never the potential for success without a corresponding potential for failure. When you take the right risks, though, you benefit whether you succeed or fail, because failure is a great teacher. If you hardly ever fail, perhaps you are taking too few risks. If your life is constantly careening out of control, perhaps you are taking too many. If your failures never so much as hurt your feelings, perhaps you should be taking bigger risks. If every risk you take puts your very life in danger, perhaps you should be taking smaller ones.

Risk is risk; it can harm you in all sorts of ways. Learn to discern between risks you should take and risks you should run from as fast as you can. Let your convictions guide you, and in time you'll figure out which are which, assuming you make it that far—life, after all, makes you no guarantees. *Choose your risks well.*

———————

All this talk of risk may sound dangerous. Should we not rather make *safety* our highest priority? That sounds noble enough. After all, nothing *bad* ever happens to those who are *safe*, does it? But if we never risk, we never succeed or fail; if we never succeed or fail, we never grow; and if we never grow, we remain infants forever.

Safety can only be guaranteed by quashing freedom. Demanding freedom for yourself is demanding the right to risk, to act unsafely should you choose to. Granting freedom to others is granting them the right to risk, to act unsafely should they choose to. The more freedom we have, the less safety, and vice versa. We simply cannot have it both ways; we must decide how much we value one at the expense of the other.

It can be tempting to judge the merits of a risk only in hindsight, by its consequences. But if the consequences are known before an action is taken, it is not a risk but a certainty. No, the merits of a risk must be judged by what is known at the time the risk is taken, regardless of the consequences. You should neither attempt to justify a bad risk because it turned out well nor regret too much a good risk that turned out badly.

I once had a student who had been sent by his family from the inner city to our small town in hopes of delivering him from a burgeoning life of crime. He was a thoroughly likable young man, with a sharp mind and an authentic personality, but he was torn between the desire for a better life and the call of the streets. Even in our safe little town, he found friends who were a poor influence on him, and I suspect he was an equally poor influence on them. A year after graduating high school, he was riding in a friend's car as they sped through a residential neighborhood when the car slid on a patch of wet leaves and smashed into a tree. The driver barely escaped with his life; my former student did not. Both had taken a risk, and I'm sure it was not the first time they had taken it. It is tempting to judge these boys, or at least the driver, on the events of that one fateful day, but that wouldn't be fair. After all, it would have been impossible to know beforehand whether in a lifetime of speeding through neighborhoods they would hit a tree or a dog or a child or nothing at all. The question is whether it was a risk they could be *proud* to have taken.

Another year, another student: Immediately upon hearing *The Talk*, a boy walked up to me and said, "Mr. Davis, you inspired me today. There's a risk I've been wanting to take for a long time, and you've made me realize that I need to take it right now." I laughed and wished him the best. The following morning another of my students walked into my room exasperated with me. Her best friend had just professed his love for her, but she had no romantic interest in him, and now she worried that their friendship was in jeopardy. I attempted to make her feel better, but I wouldn't apologize for my part in the ordeal. Later that day, when the boy came to class, I expected him to be crushed, but he wasn't. He was proud of himself for having taken the risk, and he remained optimistic that he could win the girl's heart in time. A few months later, his persistence was rewarded, and the two began dating. I have no idea if they're still together, but that's not the point. Had he never had the courage to express his true feelings, he would never have known whether she shared them, and he would have always wondered what might have been. He chose instead to embrace the risk, whatever the outcome, because it was a risk he could be proud to have taken.

So, I ask: *What risks would you be proud to take?*

Time

Time is our most precious commodity. Money? A measure of time spent in productive labor. Material possessions? What we use our time to obtain. Reputation? A measure of the time spent cultivating it. Potential? A measure of what we could do with the time we have left. Relationships? The reward for time spent with others. Well-being? The result of time spent caring for ourselves.

Imagine the deaths of two people, one a wealthy man of seventy, the other a poor man of seventeen. When the young man dies, we lament, "He had his whole life in front of him!" But what is there to lament when the old man dies? Not much. His wealth remains, to be divided among those he leaves behind. It is the young man's death we lament, even if he had no wealth to speak of, because he has lost something much more precious than wealth. He has lost his potentiality. He has lost all he might have done or been. He has lost time.

Perhaps the only thing we might legitimately lament in an old man's death would be his failure to have used his time well, his squandering of the potential he once possessed. Were we to celebrate his life, we could celebrate only his wise use of his time, his shrewd stewardship of that most precious resource. The young man's death, by contrast, is tragic regardless, because he loses in one lump sum all the time he never had the opportunity to spend. To a rich old man, a poor young man has wealth beyond imagining. What man at the end of his life wouldn't give every possession he had to become young again? And what poor young man has ever wished he were rich and old? A young man may envy an old man's wealth, but would he willingly part with the remaining years of his youth to obtain it? Not a chance. Even a great fool would never make such an exchange.

The young instead regard the old with pity: "See how weak are their bodies and minds, how pathetic their successes, how meager their accomplishments! Such a tragedy will never occur to me. I will achieve greatness without ever growing old. I will beat time and cheat death."

The great lie of youth: that it will last.

I have already outlived many of my former students, young people who felt exactly this way. How do I know they felt this way? Because when I was young *I* felt this way; because we *all* feel this way when we are young, *because* we are young. We all believe the great lie of youth.

None of us have much time, and none of us know how much we have. Our accomplishments rarely reach our aspirations, and only once we have passed the pinnacle of our faculties much sooner than we expected do we realize what a precious commodity we have been spending all along. *Then* we cling to it, hoping, if we cannot prevent our inevitable decline, to at least prolong it as long as possible. Only then do we realize that we too will grow old, that we will not accomplish so very much, that we will not beat time, that we will not cheat death.

When the young die, we often say they are "gone too soon" or have "died before their time." Really! As if we all deserve some generous allotment! As if the dead have been cheated! Life itself is a fleeting gift with no guarantees except that it is destined to abandon us in rather short order. How soon is too soon? How much time do we *deserve*? Such questions are born out of hubris. The only real question, the question that demands an answer from each of us every day, is what we will do with the time we have left.

When our time is well spent, we love life. When it is ill-spent, we hate it. Indeed, when people take their own lives, what they are saying is, "My time on earth is so unbearable that I wish I had none left." Why does the story of Sisyphus so haunt us? Being compelled to roll a rock up a hill only to watch it roll down again, endlessly, seems an unimaginable torment to us. But why? Sisyphus lives forever! Why pity him? Because his work is for naught, because his labor avails him nothing. How do you kill an immortal? Steal his time from him, not all in one stroke but in tiny increments of waste, each moment lived knowing there is no point to his existence. Condemn him to spill his time out on a hill, forever, and you condemn him to die, forever.

It is easy to say that time is precious, but do we act like it? Every one of us sacrifices it at the same rate; our only choice is how we sacrifice it. Why study for your exams rather than go out with your friends? Because you believe that sacrificing time with your friends in the present will yield a better return on your time in the future. Why go out with your friends rather than study for your exams? Because you believe that being with your friends in the present is a better use of your time than investing it in an uncertain future. Regardless, one way or another, your time is relentlessly spent. Tick... tock...

How might you extend the potentiality of your time? One way is by doing things in the present that positively impact the amount of time you have left. By living a healthy lifestyle or avoiding dangerous things, for example, you may improve your odds of having more time, though there's no guarantee. You could also invest your time in things that will remain after you are dead and gone. You might, for example, erect a building or create a land trust that will remain intact for decades or even centuries after you die. You might acquire wealth that could be handed down to those you care about. You might build up a reputation that will live in people's memories after you're gone. You might invest your time in people younger than yourself.

How ought you to spend your time? Those in the best position to help you answer that question are those nearest death, those who have spent almost all their time already. What do they most celebrate having used it for? What do they most regret having spent it on? What do they wish they'd done with it now that it's gone? You may find it a wise investment of a little of your time to ask those nearest death these questions. In all likelihood, they would be grateful for your curiosity, seeing in you an opportunity to multiply the potentiality of their remaining time, to invest some of the little they have left in one who likely has more.

I asked these questions of my mother when she was seventy-six years old. What time did she most celebrate? The time she'd spent with her children, the best times of her life. What time did she most regret? Time spent working. What did she wish she'd spent more time doing? She wished she'd had the means, as her mother had had, to hire a live-in servant so she could have spent more time with her family. But she'd had to be realistic. She'd worked two jobs while her children were growing up to provide them with opportunities she'd never had. She'd not gotten everything she'd wished for, but she'd done what she could with the time she'd had.

The young never fully appreciate what they mean to the old until they are old. Why do your parents and grandparents so concern themselves with you? Why do you and your future mean so much to them? Because you represent the sum total of everything they've ever worked for, their very reason for being; because you are what is left of every moment of time they've ever spent, every moment of time every ancestor you've ever had has ever spent; because you represent their only hope for a future that slips away from them with each passing moment; because you represent the only chance they have that any part of them will last.

———————

Cherish the past. Prepare for the future. Live in the present.

One of the tragedies of becoming an adult is that we so easily forget what it was like to be a child. I remember as a child puzzling over this mystery. As a child, I had no way of knowing what it was like to be an adult, but how could it be that adults so misunderstood children? Had they not once been children themselves? I resolved that this would never happen to me, that I would never forget what it was like to be a child.

What I did not realize then, with so brief and recent a past to remember, was how easy it is to forget. I recall as a young man being annoyed whenever some fool with a camera would interrupt an otherwise enjoyable gathering to force everyone to take a picture. What need was there to document every event in life? If something was worth remembering, I would remember it! But I was wrong. I don't remember. I can't remember. Memory is a fickle thing, and it becomes all the more perplexing as we age. When we're young, we think our memories are preserved in a vault for all eternity, but our minds betray us as we age. Our memories are more like homemade signs left out in the sun and rain. Without a fresh coat of paint now and then they fade to nothing, so many pieces of rotted wood lost in a tangle of vines.

I am humbler about my memory now than I once was, and I am

grateful for those who have documented my past in spite of my objections. Document your life as you go, because you will likely not remember nearly as much of it as you think you will. Guard the treasure of your childhood most carefully, lest you become an adult who remembers nothing but being an adult.

The past is your only teacher. You can multiply what you learn from it by studying the pasts of others, but the past is still your only guide. Pay attention to it. Think on it often. Let its lessons soak into you. Cherish it regardless of whether it has been kind to you or cruel, remembering that our harshest teachers are also often our best.

Cherish the past; prepare for the future. The future represents pure potentiality, that which *could be*. The thought of it makes our imaginations soar and plummet, spawning in us our loftiest hopes and deepest fears. To realize a particular future, you must make the right sacrifices in faith that you will be rewarded for having made them. The only reason you would make things more difficult for yourself in the present is that you believe that by doing so you will obtain something better in the future than you would by using your present in some other way. As a youth, for example, you are encouraged and even compelled to invest two decades of the sweetest years of your life studying things you may not even care to know. Were there no payoff in the future, studying in the present would only be done by those who very much enjoy it for its own sake. But that is a small minority of people, and even those who enjoy studying find some subjects onerous or tedious. Is spending all those years studying a good sacrifice for you? It had better be, to sacrifice your precious present for it.

Every sacrifice will not succeed. A faith in our sacrifices may more accurately be described as a faith in the *aggregate* of our sacrifices. A sacrifice is a gamble, and with every gamble there is a chance the future won't favor us. What we are really doing when we sacrifice, then, is making the best gamble we can under the circumstances. When a boy walks across a crowded room to introduce himself to a pretty girl, he knows his odds are low, but he has deemed the potential gain worth the risk, so he does it anyway. Perhaps the first and second and tenth times he makes such a gamble he will lose, but he persists in the belief that, while he may lose *this* time, he will not lose *every* time.

Eventually, he will win, and when he does, it will more than offset the sum of his losses.

Cherish the past and prepare for the future, but live in the present. In reality, you have no choice, because the present is all you have; it is all that exists. The past *did* exist and the future *will* exist, but only the present *exists*. You may treat the past and future as realities, but they are only realities in your memory and imagination. The only moment in which you can act is *now*. Even your thoughts of the past or the future are merely figments of your brain activity in the present. You can do nothing about the past, and the future is elusive. The only thing you can control is the present, and even then you have limited control. *Use your control well.*

You can't live in the past or future, so why try to? To do so is to miss what the present has to offer, to refuse to accept life for what it is *right now*. Don't be in a rush to bring the future into the present. Right now, you are what you are. Don't be in a hurry to forfeit the remaining years of your youth to become an adult; you will become your future self in due time. Be grateful instead for who you are *right now*, for the season you are in *right now*, for the blessings and obstacles and opportunities you have *right now*, and accept your future as it becomes your present, treasuring each moment as it comes and goes.

When you are young, you inhabit a world of endless possibilities. But the future becomes the present and the present becomes the past every moment of every day. Whenever you choose to use your time to do a thing, you do it to the exclusion of every other imaginable thing. You have the potential to do a great many things, but you cannot do *all of them*. With each passing moment, an infinity of potentialities become just one reality, your life narrowing with each tick of the clock.

Consider, then, based on your tendencies, what you would be most likely to regret as you approached the end of your life. Perhaps you tend toward laziness and someday might wish you'd worked harder. Perhaps you tend toward ambition and might wish you'd achieved less and enjoyed more. Perhaps you tend toward selfishness and might wish you'd invested more in others, or toward selflessness and might wish you'd invested more in yourself. Perhaps you tend toward carelessness and might wish you'd been more careful, or toward carefulness and might wish you'd been more careless. Whatever your tendencies, stop and consider what you are most likely to regret about them, and then do something in the present to make sure that when you reach the end of your life you will be able to say you have spent your time well.

When you know who you are and have taken proper aim, you free yourself to embrace the present for whatever it has to offer: every joy and every triumph, every sorrow and every defeat; every clear mountain vista, every rainy day, every ray of sunshine, every biting wind; every mundane task, every increment of progress, every setback, every searing pain; every moment with those you love and every moment without them. Living in the present means being fully engaged in life, every moment of every day. What more could you ask than that?

So, I ask: *When you reach the end of your life, how are you likely to wish you had spent your time?*

The Good Life

What is the good life?

For many years I taught my students hard lessons in preparation for life because I believed life to be inherently hard. But as the years progressed, and I witnessed more and more of them enabled to live in perpetual ease, I began doubting that premise. I began to wonder if I had gotten it wrong. Sure, life was hard for some, perhaps even for most, but was it necessarily hard for all? Could not at least a select few of us achieve such a level of affluence that our lives would never be hard?

We humans are naturally inclined to seek ways to make our lives easier. We develop tools and technologies to make things run smoother and more efficiently. We establish political systems, rules, and habits to make ourselves more secure. We scrub away risk and adversity until there is precious little to make us uneasy, and then we scrub some more, our lives lived somewhere in a continual progression toward the comfortable.

Suppose, on this continuum of ease, that you are particularly blessed. Suppose you have parents who perpetually enable you to suckle at your mother's breast while your father brings home a steady paycheck. Would life ever be hard for *you*? Perhaps not. Perhaps all I once thought true about identity and vision and goals and risk simply don't apply to everyone. Perhaps such ideas represent an antiquated past being continually replaced by an ever-brighter future. Perhaps some of us could afford to live in the ease of perpetual infancy. The thought nagged at me for years.

Eventually, though, I came to realize that all the ways we make our lives easier just disguise an undeniable truth: Life really is hard. It really is tragic. In spite of our best attempts to soften its blows, it threatens to undo us at every turn, and those who think it can't or it won't are those most susceptible to its cruelties. If you think life will always be easy, give it time.

Time: life's inexorable weapon of humiliation. With every beat of our hearts, with every breath that filters through our lungs, we inch closer to inevitable death. Life will kill us all. How it kills us may be slow or quick, racked with pain or fully anesthetized, but it will kill us all, and we know it. It is this knowledge that haunts us in the light, that pursues us like a shadow and whispers in our ears, "All must die. *You* will die." Life is hard because it cannot last, because it must not last. Its very definition is that which lies tenuously between nonexistence and nonexistence.

Every cell in your body conspires to give rise to another life, to pass along a seed that will last a little longer than your own, long enough to create another seed, just as your parents' cells conspired to create you. In that sense, your life has existed since life began, moving from seed to seed to seed, tracing a line deep into the distant past. But there are lines all around you: lines that converge, lines that branch out, and lines that cease altogether, forever. *Your* life, *this* life, is merely the vessel of the present, the tip of a single branch. We are terrified by *this* life because it is the only one we know we have, and it is dying from the moment it is birthed. While it lives, a vessel has no certain knowledge of what becomes of a broken vessel, whether there is, besides the seed it strives to leave behind, any life beyond this life.

Yet, even as this life ends for one of us, it goes on for those of us who remain. You are one of these fortunate few, as am I, for now. As we walk out of the funeral parlor, we hear the bees buzzing about the flowers. We feel the warmth of the sun and the gentleness of the breeze as it brings fresh scents to our noses. A woman down the street fills her car with gas, oblivious to the life that is no more. That woman is everyone in the world who does not know. For the few of us who do know, our memory is sharp at first and slowly dulls, until all that remains of the one who once lived is a vague notion, a caricature in the minds of the living. As long as we live, we may still hear his voice or smell her perfume, but the more time passes, the less sure we can be that we remember even those things correctly. At last our own memory dies, just as the memories of those who died before us died with them, and the memories of those before them, on and on in an endless stream of the forgetful and the forgotten. Nothing remains, and yet nothing changes. Today is not so different from yesterday, yesterday not so different from the day before. Thousands die and thousands are born, and the bees buzz on.

What happens, though, when it is Mother who dies, when death comes to the one at whose breast you suckled? What happens when it is Father who dies, when death comes to the one who paid for your crib and pajamas? What happens when *you* become Mother or Father? What about that day terrifies you? Whatever *that* is, that is what binds you to your infancy.

So, I ask: *What binds you to your infancy?*

Even if you were enabled to live a life devoid of pain and full of pleasure, a life of having your needs and wants met without effort or reciprocation, you would likely not find it good for long. No matter how tasty your mother's milk, you would eventually hunger for something more. That hunger is called *ambition*. It is what makes you want to stretch your arms and legs and ready yourself for action. It is what compels you to leave Mother and Father to do something of your own—perhaps even what you were made to do. You exist to be cared for only to a point, and with a purpose: that one day you might care for others. There are many ways to realize that purpose, but that is where the good life is to be found, in doing the very thing you were made to do. As you are being cared for, then, pay attention; learn. Those caring for you are showing you your purpose; they are teaching you how to aim your ambition.

Ambition is only as good as its aim. Aim for the wrong things, and your ambition will become an obsession that brings you discontentment even when you achieve your ends. Aim for the right things, and your ambition will become a passion that brings you contentment even when what you reach for eludes you. What is the aim of *your* ambition? Answer poorly and you will watch all your efforts turn to dust; answer well and you will find meaning in all you do. *Aim well.*

Ambition will drive you to focused action, focused action to success. Success will draw people to you to pay homage, and they, in turn, will introduce you to two of life's great specters: wealth and fame. Whether or not you aim for them, you will be forced to contend with them.

Wealth matters—you need a certain measure of it just to survive—but it also has a way of horning in on your aim; it threatens to dominate your thoughts whether you have too little of it or too much. You must continually ask of it, then, whether it is a means to an end or the end itself, and if only a means to an end, then to *what end*? Accruing wealth for the sake of accruing wealth is the behavior of an addict. Addiction, regardless of its object, leaves the addict perpetually discontented, degrading both by privation and excess. No matter how much he has, the addict never has enough. Do you control your wealth, or does it control you? Do you have enough? How much is enough?

Buy a big house and you must worry about maintaining and cleaning it. Get an expensive car and you must worry about its being damaged or stolen. Risk your money in investments and you must worry about being swindled or unlucky. It may seem like wealth should give you less to worry about, but it may instead give you more, because the more you have, the more you have to lose. Wealth can liberate, but it can also imprison. Beware of spending your life building for yourself an elaborate cell, lest it become a tomb you occupy sooner rather than later.

Then there's fame. Fame can be alluring, but most of us aren't built for fame. Would you rather stand out from the crowd or fit in? Most of us would rather fit in. How do I know? Because otherwise there would be no crowd.

I have actually achieved a modest level of fame. I create artwork that is well-known within a small community of passionate people. I've had perfect strangers come up to me and exclaim, "Oh, I know all about you!" That's both flattering and unsettling, to think that there are strangers out there who know all about me. That's all fame is, being known by people you don't know, and what's so great about that? No one appreciates anonymity as much as those who have lost it, and you only get to lose it once.

Thankfully, most of us will never have to worry about being particularly famous, but all of us enjoy *recognition*, a lesser version of fame. We all want to be thought creative or insightful or skilled. But why should it matter to us whether others think us those things? Is it not enough just to *be* creative? Why do we look to others to affirm it? Because we are insecure; because we are unsure of who we are and rely on others to tell us. How do we know how we're doing? By measuring our actions against the reactions of others. But the better we know who we are, the less beholden we become to the recognition of others and the more discerning we can be about whose recognition we seek.

If there is so much about fame that is undesirable, then why do we so desire it? Because we desire to *matter*, because we want to be someone others recognize as *important*. But it's more than that. It is not enough just to be known; we want to be known for the *right* things. No one aspires to be *infamous*, to be known for the *wrong* things. What we want is to be *great*, and in that sense there is nothing wrong with fame. Fame, like wealth, is a natural result of doing something exceptionally well. What we must be careful not to do is confuse the effect with the cause. Wealth and fame may be consequences of success, but they are not success itself. You want to be great? Great. *Why?*

So, I ask: *How do you define the good life? What is the aim of your ambition? What is the measure of your success?*

Hard Things

We all believe we are good and serve the good. If we didn't, we would do something else. But we believe more than that. We believe each action we take is the *highest possible good* under the circumstances. I was struck by this fact one day when I was buying buttons for my son's baseball pants. As I walked through the fabric store parking lot, I suddenly realized I was doing the most important thing in the world to me at that moment.

Repairing baseball pants is a mundane task, but if I didn't do it, my son wouldn't have baseball pants to wear. That may sound trivial, but at that moment it was not trivial at all; it was the single most important thing in the world to me. If on the way to the store I had instead decided to stop off at a bar and blow my money on alcohol, or go fishing, or leave my family and move to Acapulco, I could have done so. But my actual actions proved that each of these alternative actions represented lesser goods to me, or perhaps not goods at all. Likewise, I could have used that time to donate blood, or raise awareness for a political cause, or fly to Africa to serve in an orphanage, but I didn't. I was at a fabric store, buying buttons for baseball pants.

Whatever you find yourself doing at any moment is the most important thing in the world to you at that moment. Whether you are saving someone from drowning, gossiping about a friend, or picking your nose, every action is a testament to what you think is the highest possible good.

One time a student walked into my classroom, threw herself into her chair, and announced, "Ugh. I wish I didn't have to be here." I said, "There's the door. No one is keeping you from walking out of it and doing whatever you want." Jumping up, she said with suspicious enthusiasm, "Seriously? Are you giving me permission to leave?" I said, "What do you need my permission for? I thought you said you wished you could be doing what *you* wanted to do." She looked around at her classmates and said, "But if I leave, you'll write me up, right?" "Yes. But why should that stop you from doing what you want?" Exasperated, she said, "Because I don't want a detention!" I said, "So, what you actually want is to stay here?" Throwing herself back into her chair, she rolled her eyes and said, "I guess so." "Well," I said, "then what are you complaining about? You're getting to do exactly what you want!"

I could have let it end there and just started class, but instead I opened up the matter for general discussion. My students affirmed that none of them had ever been physically made to do anything against their will. That meant that everything they had ever done was exactly what they wanted to do! We worked our way through why the girl had chosen not to leave my class. She had said it was because she didn't want a detention. But couldn't she have just skipped the detention and any subsequent consequence the school doled out? Ah, but if she refused all consequences, she would eventually be expelled. But wouldn't expulsion simply mean she would never have to go to school again, making it all the easier to do whatever she wanted? Ah, but without schooling she would not be able to get a very good job. But why would she want a job anyway? Wasn't a job just another example of having to do what someone else wanted her to do? Ah, but without a job she wouldn't be able to buy food or clothes or a house or a car or a phone, and those were things she wanted to have. So, she *chose* to go to school day after day and do her homework day after day rather than do all the other things she might have done with her time. It was her choice all along.

Every action represents a choice. But if that's true, why do we choose to do hard things? Why not just fill our lives with endless pleasure? When I go for a run and find myself gasping for every breath, I am *choosing* to do it. But why would I put myself through such agony? Why not instead choose to sit on my couch and eat potato chips? The easy answer is that I am striving for a greater good that will come from persevering through the pain. Maybe I want a stronger or better-looking body. Maybe I believe that doing strenuous exercise will improve the overall quality of my life or even extend my life. Maybe I hope to develop perseverance to steel my body and mind for future challenges. Maybe I enjoy the sense of accomplishment that comes from having done a little better today than I did yesterday or just from giving it my all. There are all sorts of rewards for choosing to do hard things.

I would suggest, though, that there is a more fundamental reason to do hard things: *because* they are hard; because easy things don't beckon to us like hard things do. Easy things do not call us to great action, because they are too easy to require great action. Things worthy of great action are, by definition, hard.

Even into my forties, a part of me always resisted taking on leadership roles. Whenever I considered them, feelings of inadequacy and unworthiness would well up within me. I am by no means a perfect person, and it was easy to see myself as too flawed and broken to lead others. I feared that if I did try to lead, I would have to pretend to be someone I wasn't and would eventually be exposed as a fraud. Life, however, kept nudging leadership roles my way. Eventually, I came to the point that, while I still felt unworthy to lead, I *wanted* to be worthy of it. But how would I ever become worthy of leading? By leading. I acted toward my aspiration, and action begot ability. Ability was not the precursor to success; action was. My capacity to do harder things sprang to life the moment I began doing them.

Are you afraid to take on hard things because of the expectations it would create? Are you afraid of aspiring to become more than you are? Not trying is always easier than trying. Setting an expectation is always harder than setting no expectation, because setting an expectation comes with a risk, and the higher the expectation, the greater the risk. But all that comes of not trying is confirmation that you will never amount to much. Don't fear high expectations; embrace them. Choose to do hard things.

So, I ask: *Do you choose to do hard things? Why?*

Calling

When you take dead aim at your legacy and establish clear goals for yourself, you run the risk of becoming too future-focused and adopting too linear a view of life. You live in a vast, chaotic world, and your perspective and influence are puny by comparison. How could you be sure that any aim you take is a good aim? And even if your aim is good, do you really believe that by sheer force of will you will be able to bend the cosmos to your designs? Learn to mock your influence on the world or wait for the world to do it for you; you won't have to wait long.

I used the analogy before of a marksman, but it may be more accurate to see yourself as a ship captain. Taking aim is less like peering through a high-powered scope at a bullseye on a distant target and more like setting sail for a point on the horizon, beyond which lie things you can only vaguely imagine. You are not adrift without sail or rudder, but the unpredictable world around you precludes you from seeing your final destination or traveling in a straight line. You'll need to approach the journey with a combination of purpose and humility. You'll need to know where you intend to go, but you'll also need to navigate winds and currents to maintain your course, using rather than fighting them as you tack your way through life.

Your ship is only as sturdy as your principles and convictions, so construct it with integrity. At the same time, don't delude yourself into thinking you have the best principles and convictions. Remember, you are a tiny speck on a tiny speck in a vast cosmic wilderness—what could you possibly know for certain? Be humble enough to admit that your principles and convictions are just the best you have for now and that you may find better materials along the way with which to construct your vessel. You don't have the luxury of having a perfect ship or the whole journey figured out before you begin, but begin you must, because life doesn't wait. Sit around too long thinking about how to begin and you'll consume all your provisions while your ship rots in the harbor.

But why set sail in the first place? Why leave the comfort of the harbor? Because you are a ship captain, and a ship captain sails. A ship captain is beckoned. He responds to a call, a call to something *out there* that he cannot ignore. To be called is to be drawn by something outside yourself, something bigger than yourself. You do not choose a calling; it chooses you. The only choice you have is how to respond.

A calling is a call to action. It requires preparation and conviction. It requires work. Still, it is not a job. It is, rather, a *vocation*, something that *vocalizes* to you and compels you to act. A job is something you *do*; a calling is something you were *made* to do. You are unique, and you are uniquely positioned to do things in this world that no one else is positioned to do. You may not have the power to do *anything* or *everything* you would like, but you do have the power to do *something*. What is it you were made to do? Something outside you vocalizes to you. It whispers in your ear. What does it say?

Have you ever been called out of yourself? Perhaps you have. Perhaps you know exactly what I'm talking about. Or, perhaps you have never heard a calling. Perhaps you do not even know what a calling sounds like.

It is impossible to hear a call if you're not listening. How well do you listen? Do you know how to do it at all? In the modern world, we are continually bombarded with a cloud of chaos and distraction. To hear life's call, you must extract yourself from the noise and listen with intention. How well do you do that? When you find yourself in a noiseless place, do you close your eyes and listen or do you get anxious and seek out noise to fill the silence? Perhaps you need to spend less time being distracted and more time listening.

Perhaps you need to spend less time being distracted and more time listening.

Take time to quiet yourself regularly. Even if you're not a religious person, *especially* if you're not a religious person, make it a part of your routine. Take time to go out into nature alone, allowing its serenity to wash over you. Take time when you are lying in your room, or waiting for the bus, or watching children play, or driving in your car, or sitting on your porch, or listening to music, to absorb the world and allow yourself to be absorbed by it. You may be surprised how often in these times you are struck by something you would otherwise have missed. You can't conjure up moments of clarity at will, but you can make a habit of quieting yourself and giving them the opportunity to occur.

Consult a mentor, someone willing to evaluate you more honestly than you might evaluate yourself, someone willing to tell you what you need to hear whether or not you want to hear it. If you need a mentor, don't be too proud to seek one out. At the same time, don't expect more from a mentor than you should. A mentor does not give you your calling; a mentor helps you train your ear so you can hear a calling for yourself.

An essential part of figuring out who you are is taking your eyes off yourself and seeing everything that is *not* you. With eyes turned outward and ears unhindered by noise, you are properly positioned to receive a calling. But beware. The more you look outwardly, the more intense may become your desire to transform yourself inwardly. We all have the potential to change as we go through life, to become a new person all the time. We initiate some of that change ourselves, but much of it is dictated by the ever-changing circumstances life puts before us. When your boss asks you to take on a greater role, or when you have a baby born with a disability, or when your neighborhood is destroyed in a flood, or when you notice for the first time the look in the eyes of a homeless person, you may suddenly find yourself overwhelmed by a desire to become something you are not. That's a calling.

A calling pulls you out of yourself. It shows you the world in such a way that you see yourself and your place in it in a new way. Forget yourself, and you may just find what you were made to be and do. It is a mysterious transaction, the loss of yourself to gain yourself. Only by giving yourself up can you understand the wisdom in it.

So, I ask: *What calls to you from without that compels you to change who you are within?*

Entertainment

Most of us would say we wish to live a meaningful life. But why? Why do we crave meaning? Because the alternative is meaninglessness! But is meaninglessness so bad? What if we had the resources to live a completely meaningless life full of pleasure and devoid of pain? Would we not be happy? Something deep within tells us no. Something tells us that such a life would be pathetic and worthless, that it would be even worse than worthless, that the only way we could live such a life would be on the backs of many less fortunate souls who would be forced to suffer for our comfort. Something tells us, moreover, that we owe it to the less fortunate to do something on their behalf. What is it that tells us these things? Some would call it the voice of God, others the voice of society, others the voice of conscience. Regardless of its source, the voice calls to us all and demands a response.

You have but one life, its seconds ever ticking away toward its inescapable conclusion. You cannot hear the call and respond by sitting idle. You must answer the question: What should I spend my life *doing*?

Being entertained. At least that's how most of us spend our discretionary time, being entertained into oblivion. We cloister ourselves within our own personal entertainment bubbles to fritter away our precious moments being mildly amused by a constant stream of pixels and sound bites. We exchange the discipline of quiet reflection for noise. We trade real experience for virtual experience, our own imagination for the fantasy worlds of others. We trade real life for fake life until we struggle to discern which is which. We reduce our identities to profiles and our feelings to emoticons.

Perhaps that assessment is heavy-handed. Entertainment is, after all, an important part of life. Games of strategy hone our minds. Sports hone our bodies and mettle. Socializing connects us with others, building intimacy and community. Music and art enable us to experience the transcendent. Entertainment is not necessarily evil. It is, however, seductive and addictive. It can easily become an end unto itself, an end without end. It can leech away your time and potential until it is all gone, and even after your life has been spent, an infinity of entertainment will remain unexperienced, its capacity to steal away life limitless.

Ask yourself honestly whether the things that entertain you serve to build up your body, mind, and spirit or cause them to slip into lethargy, whether they connect you with others or isolate you from them, whether they make you more or less able to experience the transcendent. Be ruthless in this assessment, because those things that foster indolence also foster a tendency to justify that indolence. A lazy man often lacks the motivation to fight the very thing that has sapped him of his motivation. A man long enough sedated may no longer even realize he's being sedated, or want to.

Are we not made for more than to be entertained? Are *you* not made for more than to be entertained? Violence, disease, hunger, and thirst may be the greatest threats to *humans*, but the greatest threat to *humanity* may well be the ritual pacification of our innate desire for meaning. You *were* made for more than to be entertained, and if you are serious about living a meaningful life, you may have to do with less entertainment. That may sound dreadfully dull, but once you've begun living a more meaningful life, you may find that *life itself* becomes so interesting that you don't much miss the entertainment you've given up. Entertainment is often just a cheap way to quench our natural thirst for meaning by encouraging us to exercise passivity when we ought to act with passion. It is easier to read about a leader than to become a leader yourself. It is easier to watch great deeds performed on a screen than to do great deeds yourself. It is easier to play the hero in a game than to become a hero yourself.

Would you rather be entertained by the greatness of others or be great yourself? Meaning is not found in passivity. You must track it down with fervent pursuit and fierce endurance. Meaning must be earned.

So, I ask: *What is worthy of your fervent pursuit and fierce endurance?*

Heroes

We are all at times weak, vulnerable, and helpless. What we need is a hero, a champion, someone willing to risk much to rescue us, someone willing to take the blows meant for us and to do for us what we cannot do for ourselves.

You cannot hire a hero; a hero comes of his own volition. You cannot pay a hero; a hero comes to sacrifice. You can praise a hero, but a hero does not seek your praise. You can thank a hero, but a hero does not seek your thanks. The best way to respond to a hero is to honor him, and the best way to honor a hero is to become a hero yourself.

Who has helped you when you have been helpless? Who has done for you what you could not do for yourself, expecting nothing in return? Who has fought and sacrificed on your behalf? These are your heroes.

Maybe you feel like you've never had a hero. Maybe you feel like you've never had a champion. Maybe you feel completely alone in the world, or worse, that you live in a world full of villains. Maybe you have been victimized, and your victimization has nothing to do with you, and there is no one to save you from it. It is likely, though, that that's not entirely the case, that you are isolated in part because you choose to be isolated, that you have no heroes because you rebuff attempts others make to help you, that you see only villains because you choose to see the worst in people. If at least some of that is true, then you are at least partly responsible for your situation and haven't exhausted all possibilities for help. If you need a hero, admit it. Then look for one—they're around.

Even if a hero only saves you from immediate danger, his value goes far beyond the immediate. A hero helps you resolve the tragedy of your existence in a world that owes you nothing, not by destroying the obstacles you face but by showing you how to take them on with integrity. A hero encourages you to build yourself up until you no longer need a hero. A hero inspires you to become a hero yourself, a champion for someone else in need of a champion. It is, after all, the greatest victims who make the greatest heroes.

And it is the greatest victims who make the greatest villains. The difference between the villain and the hero is not that one has suffered while the other has not; the difference is in how they have responded to their suffering. Like the hero, the villain is invigorated by suffering, but in a bent and twisted way. A hero knows tragedy and resolves to fight on behalf of the good, even if it means being destroyed himself; a villain knows tragedy and resolves to destroy whatever good remains, even if it means destroying himself. A hero sees a broken world and sets about fixing it; a villain attempts to reduce it to ash.

We are all born to be heroes, and when we're young, we know it. Why do children yell, "Charge!" as they brandish sticks and run through the yard toward some imagined foe? Because they want to be heroes. Do they need to be taught to play this way? No, they just do it. Why? Because being a hero is the most meaningful thing they can imagine to be. One of the most wonderful things about young children is how unfettered their imaginations are by pragmatism. They see in themselves limitless potential, because reality has not yet convinced them to define themselves too narrowly. In their imaginations, they can be a knight or a nurse, a farmer or an astronaut, a firefighter or a mother, a queen or an explorer. There is always some adversary to vanquish or some adversity to overcome—some worthy thing to *do*, and someone worthy to do it *for*—else the game loses its meaning. A game without challenges is a bore, and why bother playing a boring game? For that matter, why bother doing anything? So it is with life. For the game to matter, we require that it require a hero, and children fantasize about being that hero. We all have that desire, initially.

So, what happens to it? Desire is a hunger, and it may be fed with either milk or solid food. Do you only ever experience the virtual heroism found in movies, books, and games? Being a hero in your imagination is easy, but the real world is complicated and difficult; it takes focus and endurance to be a hero there. If you aren't vigilant, the sharpness of your desire for real meaning fades, dulled by the bloodless banality of your daily life, sedated by the ritual fulfillment of your basic needs and frivolous wants, until one day the hero inside you dies a slow death of neglect, its coffin a business suit or soft pajamas.

But for the attentive, there are always opportunities to be a hero, always battles worth fighting, always those in need of a champion. Sharpen your vision, and you will begin to see them; the invisible will become visible to you.

But beware. Real hero work is not the sort that takes place in story books; it is messy, exhausting business. Real hero work often involves not isolated moments of greatness but sustained commitment over years and decades, with plenty of days along the way you'd rather forget. To be a real hero, you must put others before yourself, not only when it is convenient but as a way of life.

Hero work is dangerous. We all like to see ourselves as the conquering hero, but heroes are also vanquished—heroes fall. At the heart of a hero is sacrifice, and sacrifice means loss. No one who makes a habit of risking much finishes life undefeated. Rather than aspire to be undefeated, then, you ought to aspire to be undaunted by defeat. Let your defeats, however bitter they may be, teach you, hone you, and toughen you, but never let them deter you from the next fight.

To be a hero, you must be willing to die. That death could take several forms: the death of your pride, the death of your reputation, the death of your opportunity, the death of your relationships, or even your actual, physical death. The risks I speak of are not merely figurative; they are real, and real risks have the potential to destroy you in all sorts of ways. Are such risks worth taking? That depends on the risk. Some risks are foolish; others are exactly the right risks to take.

When people shrink back from the call to become a hero, a jealous, cowardly spirit has a tendency to spring to life in them, a spirit that relishes watching heroes fall. It is such people who are the first to pounce when a hero goes down, like wild dogs upon a wounded lion. Those who have never risked much are often invigorated by feeding on the flesh of the magnificent. Those who will never be lions themselves often find solace in becoming lion-eaters. Beware of becoming a lion-eater. When you find yourself tempted to glory in a hero's fall, ask yourself why. Ask yourself how much *you* have been willing to risk. A true hero respects anyone willing to step into that close, deadly space where heroes rise and fall.

When you lose a hero, it may feel like a great hole has opened in your life. When that happens, mourn the loss, but don't mourn in despair. Instead, see it as an opportunity to rise up and take your hero's place. Consider it your honor and privilege to become for someone else what your hero has been for you. A hero who leaves a legacy in the lives of others never really dies. When you rise up to take your hero's place, the heroic springs to life in you. No longer merely inspired by your hero, *you become the hero.*

The world is a place where terrible things often happen. What will you do about it? Will you seek out a corner in which to live out your days in safety, or will you venture out where the terrible things happen and look for someone and something worth risking everything for?

So, I ask: *What are you called to fight for? Whose hero are you called to be?*

Meaningful Things

When you have little meaning in your life, it is tempting to cry out for it by seeking the affirmation of others just as desperate as yourself. Do you find yourself exposing every detail of your life to the world in an attempt to convince yourself it has meaning? Do you feel it is a matter of general concern what you ate for breakfast, or what music you listen to, or how cute your pet is, or what opinions you have on social issues, or who you follow, or who follows you? Are you so interesting that the ordinary activities of your daily life are of general import to others? Probably not. But even if you are, the world around you is still far more interesting than you are; you are simply too limited to make it any competition. Convince yourself of that. Turn your gaze outward to the world of amazing things waiting to be discovered, experienced, and done, and you will find that a better world awaits you *out there* than any you could construct *in here*.

Cries for attention are weak attempts to find a completely self-interested form of meaning. Such attempts suffer from the hubris of believing that others exist, indeed, that the whole world exists, for *you*, for *your* benefit. It is natural to think in this way, because others have poured their lives into you since before you were born, and the world has treated you graciously, else you wouldn't exist. The hubris is born when you believe that you *deserve* such treatment. The world belongs to you, it is true, but you also belong to it, and not in equal measure. The same goes for other people. They belong to you, but in a far greater sense, you belong to them. You are a tiny part of a much larger whole. Something greater than you lays claim to you, and rightfully so.

Meaning cannot be found within. If it could, you would not need to seek it—you would already have it! No, meaning is found outside you, and you know it. You have known it since you first began seeking it. Affirm this truth not with cries for attention but with a commitment to act with integrity toward the people and world around you. Prove to them that they matter to you by the way you use your time and energy. Instead of filling your time with meaningless things and then begging others to find them meaningful, find more meaningful things to do!

But what things? Whatever calls to you! Life is full of meaningful things to do! But how do you recognize them? First, meaningful things are not self-interested; second, meaningful things are not easy. Meaningful things are burdens, and the most meaningful burdens are heavy burdens. Why do we choose to do hard things? Because anything meaningful is hard.

You do not choose every burden you must carry. Some you are born with; others are thrust upon you by circumstance. The first job you have is to carry the burdens you did not choose. Approach this task not with resentment but with anticipation, because the heavier your initial burden, the stronger you have the potential to become by carrying it. At first, your burden may be too heavy for you to carry alone; you may need others to help you. These are your heroes. Persist long enough and hard enough, though, and over time you will find your legs stabilize beneath you; you will feel your back straighten and your grip tighten; you will begin to walk taller and see farther. The transformation won't be quick or without its stumbles, but it does get easier, and when it does, the world around you will seem a smaller, less intimidating place, because you will have become bigger and stronger.

No one is called to carry his own burden. Remember, a calling calls you *out* of yourself. Learning to carry your own burden is, rather, a prerequisite for pursuing a calling. Only once you can do it unassisted will you have tasted your potential, and once you have, you will find yourself looking around for other burdens. This will require no special motivation, because those who have mastered their own burdens are always looking for more. You will begin to notice people you never noticed before, people lying exhausted under their burdens or dragging them inch by inch behind them, burdens too heavy for them but no longer too heavy for you.

Each burden that calls out to you is an opportunity for you to become someone's hero. The world, though, is full of burdens, and you are but one person; you cannot carry them all. You must find the right burden, a burden worthy of your mind, body, and spirit, a burden you would be privileged to carry. Once you have found such a burden, you will have found something meaningful to do. Then you have only to do it.

Not everyone who needs your help wants it, and not everyone who wants your help wants to help themselves. It is easy to identify the first sort, but the second is trickier, because among them are those who have mastered the craft of neediness. There are those who *need* others to do for them what they *cannot* do for themselves, but there are also those who *want* others to do for them what they *can* do for themselves. Don't help the latter. There are ample people who need your help and want to help themselves; why waste your time with those who don't and don't? The goal is not to resign such people to perpetual languishment but to force them to reevaluate themselves. By refusing to give them what they want, you may be doing for them exactly what they need. And if that doesn't help them, nothing else would, either.

Helping others is never about what you can do for them; it is always about what they can do for themselves. Don't steal away from another the quickening you felt the first time you carried your own burden unassisted. Someone may merely need to lean his burden against you for a short while so he can rest; or, he may need you to shoulder a large portion of it for a great while. Regardless, do only what is needed, never more, and over time do less and less until you render your help obsolete. That way, you encourage another's legs to strengthen, and back to straighten, and grip to tighten, that one day he might carry his own burden, and in time perhaps even the burdens of others. There is nothing more gratifying than watching someone for whom you've been a hero become a hero for someone else.

In that there is great meaning.

So, I ask: *What meaningful things call out to you?*

Discipline

A principled life is a disciplined life. Why? Because once you have principles, you must sacrifice other things to your principles. That's what it means for them to be *principles*: They occupy a principal position in your life. Once you have found your aim and have determined what sort of person you want to be, once you have accepted a calling and found something meaningful to do, there are disciplines to develop. There is work to be done.

You may as well start with your body, because it is hard to do anything with a soft, weak body. Take command of it. Get yourself into shape. Make your body your slave rather than your master. Eat well. Exercise well. Work well. Sleep well.

Getting into shape and staying that way is not equally easy for everyone. I have a friend who, when I met him in his early twenties, weighed 330 pounds. He was genetically predisposed to being heavy, but he also indulged his appetite and neglected his physical fitness. Everything changed when his first child was born. He suddenly had an intense desire to break the cycle of obesity in his family, be a good example to his children, and live to see his grandchildren. It was a serious calling requiring serious disciplines. So, he began developing them, immediately. He cut his caloric intake in half, eliminating foods he knew he had a weakness for, and began to work out twice a day with military-like precision. The regimen was difficult at first, but over time his conscious choices became healthy habits, and things got easier. Within a year, he had lost 150 pounds and was at a healthy weight for the first time in his life. It has now been many more years, and he has made the disciplined life his permanent life.

A few years ago, he ran a time that qualified him for the Boston Marathon. After telling me the news the following day, he confessed, "I decided that running 26.2 miles entitled me to treat myself, so after the race I went out with my family and had a few slices of pizza." Do you think it's easy to transform yourself from a man who could finish an entire pizza on any given evening into one who treats himself to a few slices only after having run a marathon? No, it is not easy. Every day there is and will always be a fat little kid in his mind begging to be indulged, but he has chosen to ignore that calling for a higher one. I will never be able to fully appreciate what it is like to have to maintain that level of discipline over food and exercise—those don't happen to be my struggles—but his triumph over his struggles inspires me as I wrestle with my own.

In our culture, excess is a much bigger threat to our well-being than scarcity is. In places with a scarcity problem, the poor are malnourished. Here, obesity is severest among our poor. Physical obesity, however, is just a symptom of a greater cultural problem we have with indulgence, a problem that has nothing to do with body type. Even as a skinny person, I may be just as guilty of having an indulgent mindset as a fat person is. The question is one of control. What steals your attention and dominates your thoughts? Food? Drugs? Sex? Money? Relationships? Games? Self-image? Success? Make an accounting of the ways you spend your time. Ask yourself honestly if you control each aspect of your life or if it controls you. Then take systematic command of each one, putting them in their proper places by developing disciplines designed to submit them to your will. When it comes to vices, it is either control or be controlled. There is no such thing as a harmless vice.

So, I ask: *What controls you?*

Disciplining your mind and spirit are just as important as disciplining your body, but start with your body. The mind and spirit are complex and esoteric, the body simple and mechanical. Besides, control over the physical is a powerful path to control over the psychological and spiritual. To master the body, mind and spirit must act as halter and whip. As the body toughens, it can withstand more whipping, fortifying mind and spirit. As mind and spirit strengthen, they can push the body harder. Each feeds the others, discipline in one area becoming discipline in all. The idea is not to torture yourself in perpetuity but to refine what you desire, to use what you *do* to transform what you *want* to do.

Stretch your mind with difficult work. If your calling does not sufficiently challenge your mind, find alternative means to stimulate it. After graduating from college, I worked in childcare for two years. My mind had just been trained to run mental marathons, and my first job was, mentally speaking, a casual stroll. So, I taught myself chess, learned to play the guitar, and made a study of all the words in the dictionary I thought I should know better. Edify your mind every day with strenuous mental exercise; it is every bit as important as edifying your body with strenuous physical exercise.

Challenge your spirit by setting aside time each day to quiet yourself. Quieting yourself can be something you do not just when you find it opportune but as a regular spiritual discipline. Some call this meditation, others prayer. It isn't important what you call it; what's important is that you do it. Quiet yourself as an act of humility, as a way of reminding yourself of exactly who and what you are in relation to the world around you. Clear away all clutter and busyness from your mind, and listen. Reflect on your aim, on what you seek above all else, and listen. Reflect on your relationships, on what you must forgive and seek forgiveness for, and listen. Consider what you need to do today to become a better person than you were yesterday, and listen. The more you quiet yourself, the more natural you'll find the process. Eventually, you'll find yourself quieted not just at specific times but all the time, peace and winsomeness no longer transitory states you seek but abiding aspects of who you are.

What if you cannot develop discipline because you have no discipline? Then find someone to discipline you, to train you, to push you past your false limitations. This is what makes good teachers, coaches, trainers, and spiritual mentors, that they see you not for who you are but for who you could become, that they fully expect you to become that version of yourself. Find someone like that, someone who will confront rather than coddle your weaknesses, someone who will push you to push through them to a better version of yourself that awaits on the other side.

Sound mind, body, and spirit are not ends themselves; do not lose sight of why you pursue them. It is not to look good in a mirror or to impress others. These are shallow, weak reasons to build yourself up, and the result is a caricature of a person, a puffed-up buffoon. Sound mind, body, and spirit are, rather, the well-worn tools with which you build a meaningful life. Hone them until they can perform whatever tasks you demand of them.

So, I ask: *What disciplines must you develop to hone your body? Your mind? Your spirit?*

Limitations and Strengths

Part of figuring out who you are is figuring out what you can and cannot become. Some things are not just out of your reach now but will remain out of your reach forever. You will likely never become a princess, a movie star, or a superhero. Be honest with yourself. The restrictions of life force you to let go of some dreams to reach for others, and it takes wisdom to figure out which to continue to reach for and which to let go. A dream often reflects a deep calling, so don't dismiss too readily even the most daring of them. Instead, try to discern which part of a dream is essential to who you are and hold onto that part, allowing other parts to fall away so your dream can mature into a better dream. You may never become a princess, but you may be able to use your influence to help the less fortunate. You may never become a movie star, but you may be able to express yourself in ways that move people. You may never become a superhero, but you may be able to champion the cause of justice.

Learn to tell the difference between permanent limitations and temporary limitations. Permanent limitations cannot be surmounted no matter what you do; temporary limitations represent a mere lack of vision, tenacity, or development. A temporary limitation cannot remain temporary; it is either overcome or allowed to become permanent.

If you're not sure whether a limitation is temporary or permanent, assume it is temporary. I once had a student who was inspired by her experience in my class to become a biochemist. The problem was that she was unexceptional in both chemistry and math. When she came to me to ask for a recommendation letter, I gently tried to steer her away from biochemistry toward something less rigorous. She listened until I'd finished, and then she said, "Well, I don't really care whether you think I can do it or not. I'm going to become a biochemist." Imagine! She had figured out exactly what she wanted to do, only to have the very person who had inspired her to do it advise her not to try! I have always felt bad about my part in that conversation, but perhaps it went exactly as it needed to. She had sought out trustworthy counsel; I had given her my honest opinion. Had her commitment been weak, my dissuasion would have been enough to crush her hopes and send her in another direction. Instead, it elicited from her precisely the temerity she would need if she were to have any chance of succeeding.

Listen to wise counsel, but don't blindly follow it. Strive to know yourself well enough that you become the most reliable judge of your limitations. Even then, assume you are capable of more than you think. Know your limitations, but don't know them too well.

Some limitations are more critical to address than others. Are you in the habit of saying things like, "I just don't test well," or, "I'm just bad at math," or, "I just can't spell"? Really? You don't test well? Why not? Do you struggle with reading comprehension? Is your analytical reasoning weak? Are you unable to focus for long periods of time? Do you wilt in pressure-filled situations? Any one of these is a serious deficiency; do you really think you'll skate through life without addressing it? Deficiencies like these can be addressed if you are willing to put in the work. But that's just it. People who begin sentences with "I just don't..." or "I just can't..." don't do it because they've identified a deficiency and are working hard to address it; they do it because they have given up on themselves and want others to excuse them for it. Don't excuse away your deficiencies. No one will ever be impressed by what you cannot do.

Midway through a school year, I was grading a student's assignment when I suddenly found her unable to spell simple words. When I addressed the matter with her, she blushed and said, "I'm sorry, Mr. Davis. Spelling is really hard for me, so every time I complete an assignment, I take it home and correct the spelling before I hand it in. Since you collected this assignment in class, I didn't have the chance to correct it. Would you like me to redo it?" Here was a girl who had identified a deficiency and, rather than excusing it away, had worked so hard to keep it from holding her back that I had not even recognized it was a problem for her for months. She was wise to do that, too, because there is no faster way to make someone think you're stupid than to have poor spelling or grammar and no faster way to make someone think you're smart than to have sharp spelling and grammar. The same goes for math. These things matter. Don't excuse away your deficiencies; address them.

You may never turn your deficiencies into strengths. There are those who have done it, but they are the exception rather than the rule. Don't worry about that. Address your deficiencies with tenacity, taking whatever measures are necessary to keep them from holding you back. Whether you eventually turn them into strengths or not, you will be the better for having addressed them.

Let your deficiencies propel you toward your strengths. We all love the story about the paraplegic who learns to walk again. But what about those who never learn to walk again? Are they just lazy paraplegics? What about the paraplegic who learns to walk again but never realizes her dream of becoming a ballet dancer? Is she a failure? Remember, you will not always be able to do whatever you wish or become whatever you wish, but just because you cannot do or become *one thing* does not mean you cannot do *anything* or become *something*. Someone without the use of her legs may never be able to become a ballet dancer, but she may be able to become a great violinist, or scientist, or author, or friend. I know a paraplegic who became a great *track coach*.

To achieve greatness, natural strengths are not enough; they must be cultivated with passion. The more modest your talent, the more exceptional your passion must be. That is what marks the remarkable few who turn their deficiencies into strengths: exceptional passion, the willingness to sacrifice much to a singular purpose.

The purest passion always pursues something other than self. A musician becomes great not by seeking to become a great *musician* but by fervently pursuing *music*. The greatest forget themselves in their pursuit, unhindered by and perhaps even unaware of their own greatness. What is great, after all, about doing what comes naturally? In their own eyes, the great are normal. What they are more likely to find remarkable than their own greatness is the comparative lack of passion they see in others.

You will not have time to address every limitation or develop every strength into greatness, so choose your pursuits carefully. Bear in mind, too, that life may bring you circumstances and people that supersede your plans. You may have to become content with less than greatness in your own pursuits to become more of what someone else needs you to be in theirs. Self-improvement can become a form of selfishness, the quest for greatness an idol cast in your own image. It takes a secure identity to become less so that others might become more. Embracing this transaction can itself be a form of greatness, perhaps the greatest form of it.

So, I ask: *What limitations do you need to address? What strengths do you have the passion to pursue to greatness?*

People

A doctor, a lawyer, and a politician are dropped in the wilderness to fend for themselves. If that sounds like the beginning of a bad joke, it is. We all like to project an air of power and control, yet each of us is dependent on soldiers and police for our security, farmers and truckdrivers for our food, textile workers and tailors for our clothes, treatment-plant operators and plumbers for our water, and our own mothers and fathers for our very existence. None of us are self-made, and none of us control very much. Much was given to us before we ever did anything for anyone, and even at the pinnacle of our usefulness we receive far more than we earn.

Believing that you have earned what others have done for you deceives you into devaluing people, tempting you to treat them as means to your own ends rather than as ends themselves. Treating others as means rather than ends is counter to the very principles that have enabled your existence in the first place. Were it not for every one of your ancestors having devoted themselves to the matter of creating you, you would not exist. The reason they invested their lives in you was not so you could waste your life in self-absorption but so you could invest it in others in the same way others have invested theirs in you. The mandate is not merely sociological but biological—it is written in every cell in your body. Given the choice between a life of using others or serving others, the very core of your being tells you that the former would be meaningless and the latter meaningful. You know it. You were *made* to know it.

Do you treat people as means or as ends? It's easy to tell. Just examine how you treat those of lower social status than yourself. How do you treat your little sister, or the freshman in your class, or the lunch lady in the cafeteria? How do you treat those who need you more than you need them?

What I'm not suggesting is that you just be nice to everybody.

People are often nice because they are insecure or fear conflict or want something in return. Niceness can be used to mask all sorts of toxic attitudes and intentions. Often, niceness is just a substitute for honesty, and a poor substitute it is. Don't disguise your true feelings behind social graces and then pretend the deception is a virtue. If you are in the habit of being nice, ask yourself why. Is it because you truly care about others, or do you have ulterior motives? Only by truly caring can you move beyond niceness to a deeper, better virtue: kindness.

Be just as cautious with honesty as you are with niceness. While niceness may be used to take the edge off the truth, honesty may be used to sharpen it to a point. Brutal honesty is no virtue. Those who make a habit of being brutally honest are generally more brutal than honest, and even if they dispense brutality and honesty in equal measure, it is no great virtue to be half-brutal all the time. Don't indulge in cruelty and then claim with innocence that you are only being honest. This, too, is a deception.

Because of honesty's potential for brutality, it takes courage to surround yourself with honest people. If you wish to grow, you will need to make sure you always have people in your life willing to tell you exactly the way things are rather than the way you would like them to be. In fact, a good measure of your maturity and sense of self is how brutally honest a person you can tolerate. Seek to extend grace, therefore, both when being honest and when others are honest with you. It is all too easy to extend grace to ourselves, justifying our every attitude and action, while simultaneously holding others to a less forgiving standard. Honesty should always be tempered with a double portion of humility.

Humility requires honesty just as much as honesty requires humility. False humility is simply another form of pride. How do you know if you're truly humble? Well, how easily do you laugh at yourself? Everyone likes to laugh, but no one likes being laughed at. Why? Because we take ourselves seriously and wish others to do the same. Why? Because we think more highly of ourselves than we ought to. Don't think too highly of yourself. Don't take yourself too seriously. That's a pretense, a wearing of fancy clothes. Imagine we all walked around naked. Would you still take yourself so seriously were all your inadequacies on full display? And those are just your physical inadequacies. What if your every thought were exposed, your every intention revealed for all to know? There is no need for false humility; we all have ample reason to be truly humble. A person who can laugh at himself is one who sees himself accurately, as the ridiculous farce that he is, an ape with clothes on. A person who can laugh at himself walks through life impervious to the sneers of the better-dressed apes around him because he knows himself for who and what he is.

Authentic humility makes us more tolerant of others, not to mention more tolerable to them, but that's not to say that tolerance is itself a virtue. The problem with tolerance is that none of us really believe in it. To be truly tolerant is to embrace every action as good, something none of us are prepared to do—we all have things we refuse to tolerate. Tolerance suffers from the same flaw as a virtue as intolerance does: It is lazy. One represents mindless affirmation, the other mindless condemnation. Neither demands what every true virtue requires: discretion.

A better virtue is understanding. Remember, everyone acts toward the highest possible good they can imagine in the moment, meaning everyone has good reasons for doing everything they do. Practicing understanding means investigating, pondering, and even internalizing the thoughts and impulses of others until their every action becomes perfectly reasonable to you. That doesn't mean that you must abandon your critical faculties and embrace every thought and action of others, but you must understand them before you can discern whether they warrant your tolerance or intolerance.

When you treat others as ends rather than means, when you approach them with humble honesty, when you go beyond niceness and seek to truly understand them, you lay the groundwork for authentic, healthy relationships. Treat people in this way and they will gravitate toward you, not just because they want to be *around* you but because they want to be *like* you.

So, I ask: *Do you treat others as means or ends? How authentically do you practice niceness, honesty, humility, and understanding?*

Relationships

Be wary of claiming anything as your right, because every right you claim foists upon others a responsibility, and they may not appreciate the imposition. If you claim the right not to be stolen from, then you make everyone around you responsible for not stealing from you. This may seem a perfectly reasonable right to claim in a well-functioning society, and perhaps it is, but claim every right with caution, because each one you claim adds to an ever-increasing burden on those around you.

Don't claim as a right what is really a personal preference; that's narcissism. If you express the *preference* not to be offended, someone may reply, "That's nice. I prefer anchovy ice cream." If you claim the *right* not to be offended, however, you make everyone around you responsible for not offending you. That's quite a thing to demand. How could those you meet possibly even know what might offend you? Are people to ask your permission before they say anything at all, just to be safe? There is no more sense in demanding that the world conform to your preferences than there is in demanding that every ice cream shop stock anchovy ice cream. Entitled brats demand their preferences. Don't be an entitled brat.

A hero does the exact opposite of an entitled brat. A hero claims a responsibility for himself and grants rights to others. A hero says, "No matter what it costs me, you can depend on me to do for you whatever I have committed to do." The world scoffs at inept, temporal beings who demand their rights, but it smiles on those who willingly take on responsibility. Strive to be a hero, one who accepts responsibility and grants rights, and the world will become to you a source of fulfillment rather than frustration.

Whenever you find yourself frustrated in a relationship, examine your attitude, because it's likely you've become focused on your rights rather than your responsibilities. It can be difficult to tell when this has occurred, because the habit comes with the tools to justify it: "He got this, so I should get that," or, "I did this, so she should do that." Whenever you find your thoughts drifting in this direction, stop. Determine to lay aside your rights and focus entirely on your responsibilities. How well are you meeting the other's needs? Don't just guess, ask. Then resolve to do better. Whether you do a perfect job is not the point. It is the change from one who takes to one who gives that breathes new life back into the relationship, even if the other does not immediately reciprocate. Make a habit of granting rights and embracing responsibilities, and in time you will become a hero in your relationships.

Approaching relationships in this way proves the vitality and maturity of your identity. Rather than train others not to offend you, train yourself to be slow to take offense and quick to forgive. Rather than shun criticism, embrace it and let it spur you to grow. Rather than avoid conflict, invite it and work through it. Rather than seek justice, seek reconciliation. Free yourself from the prison of resentment; live instead in open spaces.

Whenever you've offended someone, apologize, even if you did not intend to offend. And if you think the other has more to apologize for than you do? Apologize anyway, and do it first. When you apologize, explain exactly what you are sorry for having done, and stop. Don't weaken your apology by rationalizing your actions. Apologizing is an act of contrition, and there is no need to justify yourself during an act of contrition. If you were lazy or forgetful or dishonest or thoughtless, just say so. There is a beautiful irony in human interaction: We tend to think that admitting our offenses will diminish us in the eyes of others, when in fact the opposite is true: It endears us to them. When you freely and contritely admit your offenses, those who might otherwise have judged you harshly will instead rush to your defense, providing justification for you even when it isn't warranted. There will be no need to cast yourself in a favorable light; those to whom you apologize will do it for you.

When apologizing, don't say, "I didn't mean it," or, "I didn't mean to hurt you." Likely, when you did whatever you did, you did mean it, and meant it to hurt. If that's the case, just say so. Even worse is to say, "I'm sorry, but I didn't think you would take it *that way*." This is the opposite of an apology, a way of saying that the *other person* owes *you* an apology for having taken offense at whatever you're allegedly apologizing for. Just as bad is, "I'm sorry, but it makes me really angry when you do such and such." Don't be surprised when such backhanded apologies are met with the resentment they deserve. Those you apologize to know what it's like to have something to apologize for, and they will appreciate an authentic apology even if what you have done has hurt them.

Apologizing properly risks others thinking the worst of you, sometimes for things you did not do with ill intentions or perhaps did not even do at all. Don't worry about that. Let people think the worst of you if they wish. The goal of an apology is not justification but reconciliation, and reconciliation cannot be coerced. A true apology is a gift, an offering of goodwill. Taking offense, forgiving others, and apologizing well are choices you make, but that is where your choices end. You cannot control whether others take offense, apologize well, or forgive you. Take responsibility for yourself and yourself only, committing as far as you are concerned to being an agent of reconciliation. And then? Be patient. It can take time for people to accept an apology, particularly when they have been hurt or have their own offenses to apologize for.

Be as gracious when you receive as when you give. When people apologize to you, or go out of their way to serve you, or offer to pay your way, or give you a gift, accept their goodwill with humility and gratitude. Resist the urge to repay a kindness. Gifts are meant to be received, not repaid. Repaying a gift is really a way of refusing it. Don't treat relationships like accounts with deposits and withdrawals that must be budgeted and balanced. Don't say with pride that you never owed anyone anything. Making sure others always owe you more than you owe them is just a way of indebting them to you and then claiming their indebtedness as a virtue. This is not grace at all but its opposite, an attempt to assert your superiority over others. Did you change your own diapers? Drive yourself to kindergarten? Teach yourself algebra? You owe a lot to a lot of people. Admit this with humility and accept with grace whatever others give you. That is the only transaction that is needed.

At the same time, don't take advantage of others' graciousness.

Don't expect others to pay your way through life or fix your problems. Part of growing up is learning to take life's punches on the chin for yourself. You'll always need others, but don't let that make you needy. As an infant, you were a leech on society, taking everything you needed without giving anything in return, but it should not be your aspiration to remain an infant forever. Learn to fend for yourself. Life is tough, but so are you, or could be if you worked at it. Let others help you, but don't become dependent on them. Strive, rather, to become someone others can depend on.

Let the graciousness of those who have served you inspire you to become more gracious yourself, not because you feel an obligation to settle some cosmic account but because you *want to*. To be inspired is to humble yourself, to admit that you are not perfect as you are but could be more like *that* person, that you *should* be more like that person. Train yourself to recognize people who are better than you are and let them inspire you to become a better person yourself.

So, I ask: *How could you become more heroic in your relationships?*

Manhood and Womanhood

In modern societies, sex and gender are matters of great social and political consequence. But people have not lived in modern societies for long. Cities and written language have existed for less than one percent of human history, widespread human literacy only a fraction of that fraction. For an incomprehensible time before that, since long before humans ever had the tools to study the *subject* of sexuality, nature has been shaping us as sexual *beings*. So, who are we, and why are we the way we are?

Every ancestor we've ever had has successfully reproduced, each and every one of their successes a vital precursor to our existence. This is why matters of sex so dominate our lives—because they *must*, because if they didn't, we wouldn't *be*. Differences between women and men are not merely the trivial outworkings of social norms but are fundamental to our very existence, etched not only in our physical forms but in every aspect of our lives, shaping the entire way we view the world.

Who we are is largely defined by the risks we take, and women and men think very differently about risk. This is because the world is an inherently more dangerous place for a woman than it is for a man. A man has the luxury of choosing most of his risks; a woman has a great deal of her risks thrust upon her just by virtue of being a woman.

The defining risk women face is pregnancy. Reproduction may be paramount to us all, but that doesn't mean we bear the responsibility for it equally. It is women who get pregnant, not men. Pregnancy looms over a young woman like a coming storm, shaping her personality from an early age and informing every decision she makes. In fact, it begins shaping her even *before* she is born, with thousands of generations of her ancestors having conspired to equip her for the burden. The giant risk of pregnancy is intrinsic to what and who she is, an essential part of her very reason and purpose for existing.

A man can reproduce with almost no inherent commitment; a woman has no such choice. During pregnancy she becomes increasingly vulnerable as her needs grow and her mobility is compromised. If she succeeds in bringing a baby to term, she then faces the life-threatening act of giving birth. If she survives that, then she must somehow provide for both herself and her offspring, navigating a dangerous world tied to a slow, weak, careless creature completely dependent upon her for *years*. What's worse, she is genetically predisposed to take all this on willingly, the average woman having to successfully raise at least two children to adulthood just for our species to survive. A young woman may not even be consciously aware of the reasons for it, but she knows in the core of her being that she is vulnerable. It is an inextricable part of who she is, and her entire life's development prepares her to face this vulnerability.

The top priority for a young woman is therefore *security*. She intuits that the world is a dangerous place, a place where predators lurk, a place with dire consequences for poor decisions, a place in which her only chance of procreating is to be made even more vulnerable than she already is by becoming pregnant. She also has a limited timeline for reproduction, so she feels great urgency to get her life in order at a young age. For these reasons, girls tend away from unnecessary risk and toward responsibility and self-discipline.

A young man's priorities are more loosely defined, granting him *freedom*. He intuits that the world is a playground and a workshop, a place to explore and experiment, a place with tools, mechanical and human, to use to accomplish his ends. He has the potential to reproduce at any time with any number of women, so he feels less urgency to get his life in order. He must also test himself in the arena of men to win the affections of women. For these reasons, boys tend toward irresponsibility and recklessness and become safer only once they have established their manhood.

Young men thus present a conundrum to young women: They are both necessary and dangerous. A young man acting scrupulously could become a great asset to a young woman during her many years of vulnerability. A young man acting unscrupulously could take advantage of her and leave her to deal with the consequences. This is why a man seeking the affections of a woman must woo her. For him to accept her as a mate, it may be enough that she is attractive and available. If she is deficient in other areas, he always has the option of leaving her, and she would stand to lose much more than he in the transaction. A young woman cannot afford to be so cavalier. Before giving herself to a man, she must know him on a deep emotional level. Is he friend or foe? Gentleman or scoundrel? Provider or taker? One who will stand in the face of trouble or run? Choosing a mate is of little risk to a man, but it could easily be the single greatest risk a woman ever takes. A young woman is therefore wise to consider her relationships with men very, very carefully, and a young man seeking to win a woman's affection is wise to appreciate the gravity of her predicament.

While a woman's desire for security turns her attention naturally inward toward home and family, a man's desire for freedom turns his naturally outward toward the world. How, then, does a woman make proper use of a man, with all his wayward tendencies? First, she must coax him into turning his *affections* inward, into seeing her and her children as his primary ambition, the ambition that directs his every other ambition. At the same time, she must encourage him to keep his *vision* outward, to become for her a watchman, one who cares for those within by being vigilant to both dangers and opportunities without. The subtle task of a woman is to keep her man oriented in precisely this way, not only at first but indefinitely—affections inward, vision outward. As long as he remains thus aligned, he can be trusted to be of use to her and her children.

Much of the tension between men and women, coincidentally, can be traced to a failure to acknowledge these natural differences. What foolishness it is to presume that the opposite sex should see the world as we do! How often we cling to this ill-founded expectation in spite of the disappointment and frustration it brings! Nature teaches us that men and women not only *do* see the world differently but *must* see it differently. Freedom and security could not be more divergent priorities, each coming only at the expense of the other.

Relationships between men and women therefore demand compromise, a man willingly giving up his freedom to become a source of security for a woman and a woman willingly entrusting herself and her offspring to a man with the potential to betray that trust at any moment. That's the conundrum. That's the contract. A man who understands it tries to make sure his woman always feels secure, and a woman who understands it tries to give her man the freedom he requires.

———————

The only way for people to live together in large numbers is to develop institutions that reduce conflict and foster peace. To this end, structures such as government, religion, and marriage serve to reign in the natural freedoms of men and provide greater security for women, flattening the differences between the sexes. Men in society lose freedom but gain security. Women in society gain both security and freedom, because women can only be free once they are secure. While our institutions act as halters on our natural tendencies, however, we must be careful not to confuse sociological influences with biological. Whatever ripples society creates on the surface, a much greater inertia lurks beneath; powerful undercurrents stir our thoughts, feelings, and impulses.

Young women's preoccupation with security makes them prone to anxiety, to overestimating danger and underestimating their abilities. For that reason, provided they survive pregnancy, women tend to live longer, safer lives than men do. Young men are the opposite, prone to the self-assuredness that comes from underestimating danger and overestimating their abilities. They tend to take greater risks, resulting in both more lucrative successes and more spectacular failures.

Young men are truly awesome creatures, capable of the world's greatest evil and its greatest good. Young men have built cities and filled breaches with their bodies to conquer them. They have carried out genocides and spilled their blood to stop them. They have engineered machines that feed people by the thousands and others that kill them just as efficiently. Young men have been the world's most ruthless torturers and most uncompromising martyrs, its most oppressive tyrants and bravest champions, its vilest rapists and most courageous rescuers, its most notorious villains and most vaunted heroes. Young men represent both humanity's greatest threat and its greatest hope.

When it comes to women and children, young men have a nearly limitless capacity to edify or destroy. When young men fail to become what women and children need them to be, all are in peril. When they rise up to meet the challenge, all flourish. And what do women and children need men to be? Useful. Why? Because a useless man is useless! No woman or child needs a little boy trapped inside a man's body, another dependent to be cared for; they need a man worthy of the title and prepared to take on the titles of *husband* and *father*. And what marks a useful man? A useful man is strong, industrious, skilled, clever, responsible, attentive, protective, and selfless.

The charge to this generation of young men is the charge to every generation of young men: Become a useful man! Women need you to be one! Children need you to be one! The whole world needs you to be one!

With this charge comes great opportunity for young men to distinguish themselves among women. Are you an insecure young man, attracted to but intimidated by women, unsure of how to win their favor? Become a *useful* man! *That's* what women want. And once you've proven yourself useful to a woman? Continue to be useful to her! This is what is known as *commitment*, and it is a critical component of usefulness, because a woman who has found you worthy of her affections will want to make use of you for a long time.

Are you a young woman looking for a man? Be careful! They're not all useful! A young woman who clings to a useless man with the belief that she will one day make him useful deludes herself. A useless young man can be trained to become useful, but not by a woman. That's the job of men, just as it's the job of women to train up young women. A woman who tries to coerce a man into becoming useful becomes a nagging voice in his head, and no man appreciates a nagging voice. One of the worst things a woman can do to a man is continually remind him that he is less than he ought to be. There is no surer way to crush his manhood and drive him away.

It is possible, however, for a woman to *inspire* a man to become useful. When a man loves a woman enough, he will do anything for her, even become a better man. The problem is that a man cannot be made to love any more than he can be made to be useful, a cold fact many women have had to learn the hard way. The wisest thing a young woman can do when it comes to men, then, is to *be selective*. I wish I could give more hope than that, but the truth is the truth; it takes no account of whether you like it.

Parenthood

Why would a young man give up his freedom to become a husband and father? As a man matures, he begins to learn what a woman tends to understand intuitively, that to be truly useful he must be useful *on someone else's behalf*, that to be productive merely on his own behalf would be a waste of his potential and purpose, that there is no more worthy ambition than to devote his life to *this one person* and the few others who may one day spring from the union.

As men grow to embrace this calling, they become less violent and more conscientious, less preoccupied by sex and more amenable to companionship. Women recognize these changes and tend to choose men marginally older than themselves, men old enough to have become safer and more useful yet not so old as to have begun trending toward uselessness in the other direction. Women are no fools. The world is dangerous, and men are dangerous. A woman knows that to achieve security she must procure a man who, while not dangerous *to her*, is fully capable of being dangerous *on her behalf*. To a young man seeking the affections of a woman, then, the message is clear: Grow up. Become a source of security rather than a threat to it.

Men are both drawn to and intimidated by beauty. The most beautiful of women therefore tend to attract only the most self-assured of men, men prone to arrogance and self-centeredness. Beautiful women must therefore be the most discerning of women, because they are the most likely to be drawn into relationships in which they are exploited rather than appreciated. Less beautiful women may attract less attention from men, but they are also more likely to be appreciated for their personality and character.

A young man, coincidentally, is wise to prioritize a woman's personality and character, because these blossom even as physical beauty fades. Whenever he meets a woman he is attracted to, he should ask of her: Does she look first to her own needs or to the needs of others? Is she honest or deceitful? Lazy or hard-working? Easy or hard to please? Does she share similar standards to his for keeping a home? Does she share similar views on parenting and money, marriage's two greatest sources of conflict? Does she share a similar view of the world in general? Going through the grind of married life is difficult enough with someone whose personality and character mesh well with your own; trying to do it with someone fundamentally incompatible with you sets you both up to live in misery.

The reason I challenge young men to ask these questions is not because they are any less important for young women to ask but because young women generally don't need to be told to ask them. Remember, the world is a dangerous place for women, and they don't make it far without having considered the deeper qualities and motivations of men. Chances are, by the time a young man has thought to ask the first of these questions of a woman, she has already asked all of them and a dozen others of him.

Why, then, if women are so naturally leery of men, do so many end up in bad relationships? Don't they know better? Perhaps. But it is easier to find a useful woman than it is a useful man. An insecure young woman is likely to be tempted to latch on to the first man who shows her attention and then lie to herself about how useful he is. Women often possess a spectacular ability to lie to themselves about the men they love.

A young woman frustrated by her prospects may ask, "Do I really even need a man at all?" No and yes. The problem of useless men is nothing new, and women have become adept at compensating for them. But don't delude yourself into thinking that having no man is as good as having a useful man. In the absence of a useful man, a woman finds herself either childless or having to fulfill the roles of both mother and father for her children, and while a woman may be better at fulfilling both parental roles than a man is, no woman can ever be a father. A single mother may be relieved to be rid of a useless man, but she would much rather he be useful than absent. Single motherhood is nothing to celebrate.

In recent times, women have gained more freedom to be and do what they choose. Greater opportunities have come, however, with subtle pressures. A girl today may be led to believe on the one hand that she will never be a real woman until she becomes a mother and on the other that she is a failure as a woman if she becomes *only* a mother. A truly liberated, successful woman ought to have no trouble simultaneously excelling at both a demanding career and motherhood, right? And a superwoman ought to be able to do it all without a man even around to help her, right?

These are lies, and just the sort that young women who have known little responsibility are prone to believe. It is tempting to believe you can be all things to all people. Don't believe it. You cannot. You are one person. When you become a mother, the time you have in the day does not suddenly double. You do not get to exist in two places at once. Sacrifices are always made.

The model of the superwoman trivializes the most important role in all of humanity, that of raising the next generation. Should any generation fail to accomplish this task, our entire species fails. Raising the next generation must therefore be the highest priority of every generation; there is no shame in its being ours.

But if parenting is so important, then why should the brunt of it be thrust upon women? Should not fathers shoulder the load equally? Yes and no. No doubt a father's role is crucial, but women are specially equipped both physically and psychologically to nurture children better than men are, particularly when children are very young and need their most intensive care. There is simply no comparison between a mother's connection with her children and a father's. She has carried them inside her for nine months and gone through immense suffering to bring them into the world. Her identity is inextricably bound to their welfare. Not so with a father. His obligation in reproduction is minimal, and his motivation mirrors that paucity. Not only is he less capable of nurturing his children; he is also less willing. A society is in grave danger that refuses to recognize this plain reality and treats the roles of father and mother as interchangeable, or worse, farms out the raising of its children to professionals. Children need parents, not an endless string of surrogates, and when they are young, they need the direct care of a mother more than that of a father.

When I was in college, I was preparing to give a presentation at a conference when I was approached with an unusual request. An emeritus professor in our department wished to attend the conference as well, but she was confined to a wheelchair and would need someone to push her around. I agreed to do the job, feeling quite magnanimous about it, but when we arrived at the conference, I soon began to feel rather small. I watched spellbound as person after person excitedly approached this frail, demure woman, tickled to have her grant them a few moments of her time. My sense of astonishment eventually gave way to a sense of pride for having been selected to push her chair. Just being associated with her made me feel important, and I didn't even know why she was a celebrity. I would learn that only after arriving back home, when I received a note from her thanking me for my assistance at the conference. It was written on the inside cover of her autobiography.

Hers was a remarkable life. As a young woman in the 1930s, she had manifested a passion and aptitude for the sciences. She soon found herself, however, as many talented women do, facing the hard choice between family and career. Rather than attempt to become both a mother and a scientist, she chose to turn down all suitors and focus entirely on her research. At a time when women struggled to gain a fraction of the respect and opportunity afforded men, she was a success by any standard. She pioneered the use of potatoes as a staple food crop in countries on four continents. Thousands if not millions of people today live healthier lives because of the life's work of a woman whose wheelchair I would one day find myself privileged to push.

This woman was wise enough at an early age to recognize that she could not become both a great scientist and a great mother, that to try to do both would have been to sacrifice her best at either. Are you a young woman torn between career aspirations and motherhood? Don't believe the lie that you can simultaneously meet the demands of both with excellence. You cannot. The more you devote to one, the less you'll have left to devote to the other. That's the sacrifice. That's the choice. Don't believe the lie that you are a failure as a woman if you never become a mother. Don't believe the lie that if you are *only* a mother you are somehow inferior to career women. Heed your calling, weigh the sacrifices of your choices honestly, and then be secure enough in who you are to do what's best for you and your family, regardless of what anyone else thinks.

Men also face sacrifices when it comes to work and family, but they do not feel them as acutely as women do, because their role in bearing and raising children is not as intensive. As children transition from infancy into adolescence, however, a father's role grows. That's because mothers and fathers tend to be best at providing children with what they themselves prize most highly: women—security, and men—freedom. When they are born, children need more security than freedom: more mothering than fathering. But as they grow older, they need to be encouraged to break free of their parents and establish their independence and identity: more fathering than mothering. Nurtured too little, a child never feels loved; nurtured too much, a child never develops independence. Insufficiently mothered, a child never gets to be a child; insufficiently fathered, a child never gets to be an adult.

I hope you'll excuse these generalizations. It is not as if each sex has a monopoly on one way of being and a complete lack of the other; each of us is an individual, and we possess these tendencies not in extremes but in degrees. It is important, though, to understand our natural inclinations so we can both take advantage of them as strengths and address them as weaknesses. Women's natural desire to nurture makes them prone to indulging their children and enabling them to remain dependent too long. Men's focus on self-sufficiency makes them prone to having unrealistic expectations of their children that can exasperate and alienate them. Understanding and appreciating these differences allows women and men to work together to achieve stability in their marriage and balance in their parenting, to bind themselves not in oneness of personality but in oneness of purpose: to raise children not only to independence but to dependability, children able and willing in time to themselves care for others.

For a man, the challenge in balancing work and parenting is that the natural arc of a career often conflicts with the growth of his role as father: As his responsibilities at work increase, his growing children demand more and more of him at home. These changes squeeze his freedom, and if he's not prepared for the strain of it, he may be tempted to neglect his role at home and inflate his role at work. He may even justify the transaction as what's best *for his family*. Many a father has sacrificed his family to his career not because he has made a conscious decision to do so but simply because he has misplaced his priorities.

Children need a father to be more than a mere provider of things. A good father equips his children with the tools they need to succeed in the world and then pushes them out where they must use them. A child who never receives the tools is unprepared to become an adult, and a child who is never given the push is never forced to become one. A good father provides both, and a good mother encourages him in his efforts.

An attentive father is a source of identity, an anchor amidst life's storms, while an absent father leaves chaos in his wake. Fatherless boys are prone to wanton violence and a low view of women, fatherless girls to low self-esteem and single motherhood—fatherlessness perpetuating fatherlessness. Attentive fathers raise boys who embrace respect and responsibility and girls who have the strength and self-confidence to flourish in a dangerous world. Such men are loved by their wives and trusted by their communities. Taken on willingly, the mantle of fatherhood transforms men into better men, from aggressors into protectors, from exploiters of the weak into their defenders. Fatherhood is a man's calling of all callings; the man who embraces it becomes the very definition of useful, what every mother and child need.

Raising the next generation is the single most meaningful calling not only for this generation but for every generation. Forsake it at the peril of your children, your children's children, and the very future of humankind.

So, I ask:

> Young men: *How must you develop to become the man a woman needs you to be? To become the father a child needs you to be?*

> Young women: *How must your motherhood and career aspirations inform your decisions regarding relationships and education?*

Careers

Your initial career choice, while far from permanent, sets your life on a trajectory that influences your entire future. How do you make this choice well? First, remember that you are more than your career. A career is just one area in which you explore your calling and establish your identity. See it not as what defines you but rather as a natural extension of who you are. Don't worry about choosing poorly. If you know who you are and what sort of person you want to be, if you listen for life's call and respond to it with integrity and resolve, then you will make good choices. So, trust yourself. Don't let the magnitude of what's at stake paralyze you. Set your shoulders back and your chin square, and with eyes wide open step out in the confidence that you're ready, because you are.

I've seen hundreds of young people go out into the world with varying degrees of vision and preparedness. I've seen them go on to become PhDs and cashiers, teen mothers and tradesmen. I've seen them drop out of school and become millionaire entrepreneurs by the age of twenty, and I've seen them strung out on drugs and destitute by the same age. I've seen a lot of young people choose to do a lot of things. How do you choose well?

Choose something you like to do. This may seem obvious, but there are many people who end up not doing what they like to do. Their careers are traps. They tolerate their jobs day after day like prisoners doing time, living for the weekends until they can retire after having given the best years of their lives to jobs they hate. That's a miserable existence, and it happens for a variety of reasons: Some don't work hard enough to open the right opportunities for themselves; some enter careers for the wrong reasons, lured by romantic notions of wealth or prestige; some make poor decisions or get unlucky in other areas of life and are forced to abandon their calling for a steady paycheck; some attain the career of their dreams only to find it doesn't pay the bills or doesn't mesh well with their shifting life goals.

Choose something you like to do. Notice I didn't say choose something you *love* to do. You have no doubt heard it said, "Do what you love, and you'll never work a day in your life." That *may* be true, and it is beautiful when it *is* true, but it is not *universally* true. Consider the thing you most love to do, and ask yourself: "Would I still love doing it if I had to do it for forty hours a week, on someone else's terms, week after week, year after year, for forty years?" Maybe you would and maybe you wouldn't.

One of the things I once loved to do was create jewelry art. It was a costly enough hobby that I had to sell my work to justify doing it, so I decided to make a side business of it. It was exciting at first, but when I had to begin attending shows when I would rather have stayed home with my family, or when I had to create a piece to someone else's specifications and on their timeline, or when I went long periods without making a sale, it stopped being fun. If I'd kept it a hobby instead, I could have enjoyed it on my own terms for my entire life. Beware of turning the thing you love to do into a drudgery.

Choose something you are good at. Well, of course. Why would you choose something you are bad at? Yet people choose careers they are not good at more often than you may think, the biggest reason being that we are often poor evaluators of our own talents. Quite simply, we like to think we are better than we are at the things we like to do. What's worse, those closest to us often exacerbate our delusions by encouraging us with well-intentioned lies. That's why it's so important to surround yourself with honest people, people who care enough about you to tell you the way things are rather than the way you wish they were.

I like to play music. I have a good singing voice but play instruments with more enthusiasm than skill. Even so, I've had people tell me, "You know, you're *really* good. You should become a *professional.*" Do you know how good it feels to hear someone say that? Do you know how much you want to believe that it's true? It takes a great deal of honesty as you're walking away from that conversation to say to yourself, "That was a nice compliment, but that person doesn't know what he's talking about."

Being a performer is a lottery career, a career in which only a tiny fraction succeed. For every pop star who fills stadiums for her performances, how many thousands more toil away at their musical dreams in basements and garages? It is easy when you see someone else's name in lights to feed the false notion that *any* of us could become the one with our name in lights, that *you* could be the one with *your* name in lights. Sometimes, those with their name in lights are the worst at feeding that delusion. "Look at me," they say. "If I can do it, so can you." That's silly. All they've proven by their success is that *they* can do it, not that *you* can. There are many things others can do that you will never be able to do. We can't all have our name in lights.

You want to be the next great musician, or athlete, or dancer, or artist, or actor? Well, you may be good at it, but are you good enough to win the lottery at it? Are you a one-in-ten talent or a one-in-a-million talent? You may be good, but are you *that* good? Perhaps you *are* that good, but you simply aren't that good-*looking*, or aren't lucky enough to get the big break you need, or aren't well suited for life on the road or in the big city. Do you really want to gamble your future on all those things turning out exactly as you fantasize? Let's be honest—past a certain point, if you are still practicing your craft in your basement or garage, then what you have is a *hobby*, not a *career*. As long as you recognize it as such, there is no problem. It is when you mortgage the formative years of your life pursuing a hobby *as if it were your future career* that you set yourself up for spectacular failure. Most of us are simply not that good or that lucky. For most of us, it's a bad risk.

I have been privileged to teach at a school with a stellar music program, and I have had a few students I felt could realistically make an honest career out of music. One was a singer already performing internationally as a teenager. She was so good that the only question was whether she wanted that lifestyle. Another was a saxophone player whose passion was playing a form of jazz appreciated by very few people. He came back to see me after graduating from college with a degree in musical performance. He was by this time engaged and had begun a performing career that was paying him better than a hobby but not yet well enough to call a true career. A few minutes into our conversation, he asked abruptly, "Do you still give that talk warning your students not to pursue careers in music?" I laughed and told him I did. "Good," he said, "and if any of them won't listen to you, send them to me." He still loved performing—that wasn't his issue—but he had also begun to find out how great the sacrifices were to make a career out of what he loved to do.

What if you don't know what you're good at? How do you find out? Fortunately, you have a wealth of resources available to help you. Take a personality or strength-finding test. Many of these are free, but you can also pay to have professional counselors help you learn more about yourself and your talents and interests. Who knows? If you approached your parents and said, "I don't know what I want to do with my life, so I'd like to attend a workshop I've researched to help me figure it out," they may be so impressed that they fork over the money to send you to it. It may be the best money they put toward your education. But why should it be their responsibility? Take control of your own future and do what it takes to prepare yourself for it. If it matters that much to you, pay your own way.

Don't stop there. Find experienced people who have similar personalities to yours and are interested in similar things. Ask them thoughtful questions and listen well. One strategic conversation may be all it takes to give you the clarity you need. Find people in fields that interest you and shadow or intern with them. Invest yourself in your options until you have obtained the maturity of perspective you need to make a wise decision.

Choose something that is worth something to others. Worth can be measured in many ways, money being one of the most important. Maybe that strikes you as shallow or vulgar. Maybe you believe people should just follow their dreams and trust that money will take care of itself. That's foolishness. We're talking about careers, not hobbies, and careers pay you money. You have basic needs, and your career is what allows you to meet them. Your basic needs as a single working adult are minimal; not much of a career is required to meet them. But if you have any aspirations of having a family, and especially if you'd like your spouse to be able to stay home and care for your children, then having a career that pays a solid salary becomes essential.

For you to be satisfied in your career, though, it cannot simply bring you wealth—you must also find meaning in it, some larger purpose. The most ruthless businesspeople are wealthy beyond imagining, but does their ruthlessness give their work a sense of meaning or futility? A plumber, by contrast, gets to go home each night knowing that someone's sink no longer leaks because of the work he did that day. That's highly meaningful.

Then there are missionary careers, careers that consist in working for the benefit of others without receiving almost anything in return. The missionary life can be immensely gratifying, but it can also be demanding in the extreme. That is the sacrifice. If you choose a missionary career, make sure you know what you are signing up for: a life of poverty not only for yourself but also for any future family you may have, assuming your career even allows you to have a family. Living a life of service can be wonderful, but to live it well requires the clearest calling, the most serious commitment, the most tenacious conviction and resolve.

After college, I worked as a childcare worker in a residential treatment facility for teenage boys with severe behavioral and emotional problems. It was stressful, grueling work that paid just above minimum wage—missionary work. I had a science degree, but many of my coworkers had degrees in sociology or psychology. I did the job because I wanted to, knowing that when I tired of it, I would have no trouble finding something more financially rewarding to do. Not so for many of my coworkers. They were fresh out of college, tens of thousands of dollars in debt, and slowly coming to the realization that the epitome of their degree's earning power was to be a childcare worker in a residential treatment facility for teenage boys with severe behavioral and emotional problems. They had consigned themselves to a life of impoverished servitude, many of them without knowing it. Being a missionary can be great if it's what you've committed to do, but it's no fun waking up one day and realizing you became a missionary by accident. These same people a few years before would have told others they were studying psychology or sociology because they wanted to help people. Now they were finding out what that meant.

Choose something you like to do, choose something you are good at, and choose something that is worth something to others. Beware of careers that fulfill only two of these three criteria. If you are good at your career and it pays well but you don't like doing it, your work will become a misery to you. If you like your career and it is worth something to others but you are not good at it, your lack of ability may well hold you back. If you like your career and are good at it but it is not worth something to others, you will either be forever poor or find your work meaningless.

Choose something you like to do, choose something you are good at, and choose something that is worth something to others. Notice I keep saying *choose*. Life may call to you, but it is up to you to determine how to respond. Remember, your career is only one aspect of your calling, important but not all-important. My family is more important to me than my career, and I have a wife who feels called to be a full-time mother. If I fail to make enough money for her to stay at home or if my career demands so much of my time that I have little left for my family, then I sacrifice a higher calling to a lower one. Be watchful, because a career can easily become an entanglement, something that hinders you from higher callings. Keep your eyes, ears, and mind ever open. Life has many seasons, and each may make its own demands on your career. Strive to remain flexible enough to embrace life's changes and courageous enough to answer new callings.

So, I ask: *What do you like to do, are you good at, and is worth something to others?*

Work

Many years ago, I attended a retirement party for a teacher who taught automobile technology at my school for several decades. We sat and talked while his students, finished with their end-of-year testing, fooled around outside his shop. He lamented that so few of them were passionate about what he taught them, that while there had been a time when his students had been truly invested in the trade, most of his students now had little desire to work. He leaned back in his chair, inspected the ceiling, and said, "You know, everyone wants to make things a little easier for their kids than they had it. The problem is that, after a while, things get so easy that no one knows how to put in a damned day's work anymore."

My grandparents on my father's side grew up during the Great Depression. My grandfather, a gifted student, was from a broken family and was forced to give up his schooling in the eighth grade to go to work. He joined the army just in time for World War II and fought in some of its bloodiest battles, but he considered himself no hero; he only wished to receive some superficial wound that would get him sent home. After the war, he returned to the States and worked the night shift in a machine parts factory for decades to provide a better life for his children than he'd had. My grandmother, herself the product of a poor, broken home, worked at the same factory. As a result, my father and his sister often came home to an empty house and had to prepare dinner for themselves, but their parents' sacrifices enabled them both to attend college, the first in their family to do so. A generation later, my brothers and I grew up in the suburbs, attending good schools and receiving every opportunity to make whatever we wished out of life.

My grandparents on my mother's side were from the rough mountains of Colombia. As a young couple, they set out on horseback with their first few children and built a homestead in the jungle. Later they moved to the capital city of Bogota, where my grandfather built up a hardware business from nothing. They eventually emigrated to the United States with most of their now sixteen children, where they bought a farm and raised goats, selling milk and cheese in local groceries. When their barn burned down, killing all the goats, my grandparents, now in their sixties, moved to Mexico to become ranchers. My mother never finished high school and began working as a teenager. As a young woman, she gave up her meager savings to help send her brother, the first college graduate in her family, to medical school. Later, she worked two jobs to help provide my brothers and me with more opportunities than she'd had.

Why are these stories significant? Not because they are special but because they are *typical*. They are unique only in their particulars. They are every American story. The American story is the story of immigrants. Whether seeking a better life or bent on conquest, brought over in chains or fleeing persecution, our ancestors came. The American story is an adventure story, a story of the indomitable spirit of unlikely and sometimes reluctant heroes, people willing to quietly endure whatever they had to in hopes of creating a better life for their children. The American story is the daring dream of a dreamer, a dream realized not over months or years but over generations.

The oldest Americans we know today are of my grandparents' generation, your great-grandparents' generation, and they are almost gone. That generation grew up during some of the hardest economic times our country has ever seen, built up its infrastructure, won World War II, made incredible advancements in science and technology, and turned the United States into the most powerful economic and military force the world has ever known.

Just a few generations later our nation makes precious little, having shipped most of our manufacturing overseas. Our trade deficit, which appeared for the first time in the 1970s, grows by a half a trillion dollars a year. We consume twice as much oil as China, a nation with four times our population, and produce only half the oil we consume. We wring our hands about climate change while we maintain the most extravagant standard of living any nation our size has ever enjoyed. Never before has the American worker worked less or demanded more than he does today, his affluence propped up not by his own exploits but on the decaying remains of the economic colossus built by his parents' and grandparents' generations. Indeed, after a while, things get so easy that no one knows how to put in a damned day's work anymore.

Every four years since 1995, the TIMSS (Trends in International Mathematics and Science Study) test has been given to fourth- and eighth-graders in participating nations. Among the fifty or so nations that participate, the U.S. usually ranks around tenth. In 2007, students from China (Chinese Taipei, to be precise) participated for the first time and scored second, behind only Singapore. More telling than the test results themselves, however, may have been the responses students gave to an accompanying survey asking them to evaluate their *own* abilities in science and math. Where did Americans rank in this self-evaluation? First. Others led the world in science and math; we led the world in false confidence. In just a few generations, work ethic had been replaced with a sense of entitlement, urgency with indolence, hunger with ego. The alarm was sounded, but did anyone listen? No. Today's test results show exactly what they did in 2007—nothing has changed.

But who cares if we lead the world in science and math? Why should our generation's aspirations echo those of past generations? Ought we to be striving for economic and militaristic domination? Maybe not. Maybe we ought to be working toward other goals. Maybe we ought to be working toward providing more people with the necessities of life, or better stewarding our environment, or eliminating disease. Maybe we ought to be working toward restoring our neighborhood, or caring for the widow a few doors down, or helping someone in our family who's battling addiction. We may work at any number of things, but regardless, we must be *working*. It is what we are built to do.

The bad news is that it has never been easier to outcompete the American worker. The good news is that it has never been easier to outcompete the American worker. Even as our country's economic standing slides, even as we are outstudied and outworked by hungrier people in hungrier nations, there is ample opportunity for the willing; there is ample opportunity for *you*. Whether our *nation* succeeds may be out of your direct control, but you have no excuse if *you* do not succeed. You are a highly advantaged individual competing in a workplace rife with laziness and mediocrity. If you cannot succeed under those conditions, then under what conditions *can* you succeed?

One day my neighbor walked over as my ten-year-old son and I removed a tree stump from our yard. The reason he came over was to compliment my son, who he'd seen out there first thing in the morning, all by himself, chipping away at that stump with all the strength he could put into an axe. My neighbor had recently begun a second career as a house painter, so while my son and I worked on the stump, I asked him how business was going. "Great!" he said. "I'm not the best or the fastest painter, but I do good work at an honest price, and my customers tell me all the time how hard it is to find someone who does that. In one year, I've gone from having no work at all to having so much that I have to turn some of it away." He had figured out how to outcompete the average American worker. The formula was utterly simple: good work at an honest price.

Since 1948, when unemployment statistics began being officially tracked, the average unemployment rate in the U.S. has been just above 5%. Consider how amazing that is, to have half the people in the bottom 10% working steady jobs! Now consider the students in the bottom 10% of your high-school graduating class. Would you hire them? But wait... those aren't even the people we're talking about. The bottom 10% of your graduating class aren't the bottom 10%, because the bottom 10% aren't *graduates*. Yet even for dropouts there is plenty of work to be had if they are willing to work. If you cannot find work in America, it is certainly not for lack of opportunity.

But what about in uncertain economic times? When businesses were shut down in 2020 due to coronavirus concerns, unemployment briefly spiked to 15%. Was that not cause for panic? Maybe, for those without vision. But opportunity always abounds for those paying attention and willing to work. As dying businesses die, healthier ones rise up to take their place and thrive. So it is with people: The ill-prepared flounder while the well-prepared pioneer the future. It is critical, therefore, not only *during* difficult times but *in anticipation* of them, to have a clear vision for your future and to be working toward it.

There are many places in the world where even the industrious cannot find work that pays a livable wage, and that's with a meager definition of *livable*. Be thankful you do not live in one of those places. You live here, where even in difficult times opportunity abounds.

So, I ask: *What are you willing to work for?*

Pioneers

A recent Thanksgiving, I was sitting at the table in my uncle's home among about a dozen members of my extended family. Another family, visiting from India, were our honored guests. The conversation turned to the subject of my uncle's house, and he began detailing some of the particulars of its construction. After listening for a few minutes, the father of the visiting family stopped him. "Wait," he said, "do you mean to tell me that *you* built this house?" My uncle nodded. *"By yourself?"* My uncle smiled and said, "Well, my dad helped." Our guest marveled, "In my country I am a professor of physics, and I don't know *anyone* who has built his own house."

As it turned out, my uncle was unremarkable at our table. Another uncle had not only built his own house but designed its unique architecture as well. My cousin had drawn up the plans for his house, and his father-in-law had acted as general contractor. My father had designed and built a two-story garage with the help of a few family members and neighbors. Until this foreigner pointed it out, though, I never realized how significant that was. As an affluent member of a society with many millions of poor people, this man simply did not do manual labor; he paid others to do it for him. This was not a simple matter of laziness or elitism. In many countries, the wealthy employ the poor as a societal duty. To do manual labor yourself while there are throngs of poor people around you who could do it for you is to hoard your wealth, to rob others of the opportunity to make a living.

Americans are different. Our country was built on the exploits of the individual. We are descended from people courageous enough to have left one land for another and tenacious enough to have succeeded. I may have ancestry tracing back to Colombia, Switzerland, and Wales, but I have less in common with the people living in those nations today than I do with Americans who trace their heritage to Bosnia or Indonesia or Iran. We Americans are descended not just from people of other lands but from a certain *subset* of those people, from those willing and able to do what those who stayed behind were unwilling or unable to do. We are descended from *pioneers*, and with that heritage is ingrained in us an intrepid spirit, the desire and resolve to carve out for ourselves a home in a wild, strange land, from sheer rock if necessary. In recent decades we may have grown fat and lazy, but we are still descended from pioneers, and a pioneering spark still flickers within us.

This inquisitive, irreverent, pioneering spirit is the hallmark of our educational system, which, even in its current dilapidated state, is still in that respect the envy of the world. People flock from every corner of the globe to study at our institutions. Why? Not because we excel in book learning; other nations far exceed us in that. No, it is because we produce free thinkers. We investigate and tinker and create. We find answers to questions others do not think to ask, solutions to problems others do not know exist. We believe we can do what we cannot do, and by persisting in this irrational belief we often prove ourselves right. One of our most embarrassing traits, our false confidence, is also one of our greatest assets. The rest of the world sends us its best and brightest, hoping we will teach them to become pioneers. What they don't realize is that the people they send have already mastered the most important lesson before their feet ever touch American soil: To become a pioneer, you must leave home.

What about you? You may have grown up enjoying the fruits of the risks taken by others, but are you willing to take risks? Are you willing to leave home? Are you willing to abandon the comfort of the known for the unknown? Are you willing to continue to do it even when you fail, to make it a tenet by which you live your life? You may be descended from pioneers, but are *you* one? Look to your ancestors. Look to the foreigners who flock to our nation even today. Look to them, and let their pioneering spirit rekindle yours.

But what about Americans today? Are there any pioneers of our own left among us to inspire us? Oh, yes. The average American may no longer be a pioneer, but not every American is average. There are remarkable people all around you, people who solve today's problems and shape tomorrow's questions, people who seek each day to change the world. When you find these people, pay attention. Note their willingness to question why things are done this way and not some other way, to acknowledge that the current way may not be the best way, to try one new way after another until they discover a better way. Note the tirelessness of their work ethic, the relentlessness of their pursuit, and train yourself to see the world as they do, as a pioneer.

To be a pioneer, you need not be a great inventor or a world explorer; you need only be someone who responds relentlessly to a calling. Don't despair if that calling is modest—simple pursuits can be among the most meaningful. Being a pioneer may mean being the first kid on your street to go to college, or the first to dare not to. It may mean being the first sober person in your family. It may mean restoring something others have neglected or destroyed. It may mean trading distraction and entertainment for deeper relationships. It may mean structuring your career so you can invest greater time in your children's lives than your parents invested in yours. Examine yourself. Examine the world around you. What do you desire to be different? How badly do you desire it? What are you willing to do about it?

We all have the potential to become pioneers in our work, our families, and our communities. As we act toward that potential, we experience a curious transaction: As we better our world, we better ourselves. When we do better, we are better.

So, I ask: *How do you feel called to be a pioneer?*

How to Put in a Damned Day's Work

Before you graduate from high school, get a job, because you cannot become a full-fledged adult without knowing how to work. Work instructs and motivates everything else you do, including and especially your schooling. If you go off to college without having worked a day in your life, your ignorant mind will be fertile soil for those who wish to sow it with their own ideologies. Your original ideas, should you succeed in generating any, will come from the stunted mind of an overgrown child, and when you attempt to speak on adult topics, you simply won't know what you're talking about. Surround yourself with a host of equally ignorant peers and you're likely to emerge four years later with so many wrong ideas about the world that it could take you decades to sort them out. Being an adult means taking responsibility, something you can't know much about unless you've done it yourself. A job is not the pinnacle of responsibility, but it is a start, so if you want to begin to develop a real, mature perspective on life, get a job. Don't even worry about whether it fits your calling. Learning how to work is its own calling, an essential part of all other callings. So, get a job, any job. And then, learn how to put in a damned day's work. How do you do that?

Be humble. As a young adult, no matter how gifted you are, there is one thing you necessarily have in short supply: experience. Don't pretend to be more than you are. Instead, humbly accept that you must start at the bottom and have a long way to go before you're of much use to anyone. Be teachable. Acknowledge your mistakes. Listen. Learn.

Be curious. Curiosity fuels imagination and innovation, precious commodities in the working world. Wonder why things are done this way and not some other way. Ask questions and pay attention to the answers. Continually look for ways to improve and scale not only your own work but the work of your coworkers. Be a pioneer.

As you progress through your career, you may come to a point at which your curiosity wanes and you stop asking questions. That's a serious problem. Don't ignore it, or you may find yourself wasting years or even decades in stagnation. Ask yourself whether the deficiency lies with you or with your work. If it is with your work, then your work must change. If it is with you, then you must change. Don't be afraid to reinvent your career or yourself if you have to. Growth cannot come without change.

Be hungry. Remember, the average American worker is lazy and feels entitled to more than he deserves. If you, by contrast, are diligent and expect nothing more than what you earn, you will stand out and be given more responsibility and opportunity. Ask any boss whether he'd rather have a skilled and lazy worker or an unskilled and hungry worker, and he will take the unskilled, hungry worker every time. Why? Because a hungry worker can always be taught skills; a lazy worker will be useless forever.

Be a can-do person. Is your instinct when faced with something new to say, "I can do that," or, "I can't do that"? The first primes you for success, the second for failure. Being a can-do person is not the same as faking competence; it's merely stating with confidence that you believe you can figure things out. It's saying that you are eager to bet on yourself, that you believe you can master the things you put your mind and body to. Even if you're wrong, that's the right way to start.

Smart, competent people are can-do people, and stupid, incompetent people are can't-do people. It's not just that smart people can do more things than stupid people can *because* they're smart, though that's true enough, it's that can-do people *become* smart and can't-do people *become* stupid by the approach they take to the world. A can-do attitude spurs you into action; a can't-do attitude hobbles you, and if you've already defeated yourself before you've even wrestled with something new, how do you ever expect to learn anything? Over time, a can't-do attitude proves itself right—it makes you increasingly incompetent. If instead your instinct is to believe you can win every time, then you are at least willing to wrestle, and wrestling with all your might stands to benefit you a great deal even if you ultimately only win some and lose some. Over time, a can-do attitude also proves itself right—it makes you increasingly competent.

Have higher expectations for yourself than others have for you. This doesn't mean you must become an obsessive perfectionist, but work with integrity and strive for excellence, and you will never lack satisfied employers or customers.

My brother was once the general manager of a network of convenience stores. One day he was talking with one of his store managers when a woman approached them. "Pardon me," she said, "Which of you is the manager?" The manager identified himself and asked what he could do for her. The woman said, "I was just in the bathroom, and I have to tell you—I think that's the cleanest bathroom I have ever seen." The manager said, "Thank you, ma'am, but I think it's dirty. I was just about to go clean it again." The woman just shook her head, as amazed at his response as she had been with the bathroom. But it made perfect sense: The very reason the bathroom was so clean was that *he* thought it was dirty.

The manager, though, is not always at the store. How does he transmit those same high standards to his employees? By having done thousands of times whatever he expects them to do hundreds. It's hard not to respect and work hard for someone with that level of integrity. And who do you think my brother eventually recommended for his own position?

Be honest. Don't cheat your employer out of work, money, or supplies. Be a worker, not a clock-watcher. If you are paid to work eight hours, then make sure you *work* eight hours. Give your employer at least as much as he is paying for.

At a family reunion many years ago, I spoke with an uncle who was visiting from Mexico. He owned a ranch, and I asked him whether it worried him to leave it unsupervised while he traveled. He said, "No, and let me tell you why. Some time ago, I rewarded one of my workers with a donkey. A few days later, I called his house to ask him something, but he wasn't home. His wife explained that he was out buying hay for the donkey." My uncle shook his head. "My ranch has hundreds of bales of hay. I would never have noticed if he had taken one. And I had given him the donkey! If he had asked me for hay, I would have given him as much as he wanted. But instead, when I called his house, he was out buying his own hay." My uncle paused and raised his finger. "*That* was the moment I knew that *this* was a man I could trust. The next day, I made him my foreman, and he has been my foreman ever since. With him in charge, I worry about *nothing*."

Advocate for yourself. Don't let yourself be taken advantage of. If you think you deserve more money, or more time off, or shorter hours, then respectfully but assertively say so. If you are humble and hungry and honest, then your employer ought to respect and value you for it. Even if the conversation does not meet with immediate success, a wise employer will keep you in mind when the opportunity comes to reward or promote someone.

Of course, not every employer is wise. If your employer fails to respect a humble, hungry, honest worker who advocates for himself, then he is a fool. In that case, start looking for a better employer, and once you've found one, quit your old job and get a fresh start. Working for a fool is fine as long as you have no better options, but it is not something you should seek to do for long. Find someone to work for who appreciates you.

Treat your subordinates well. If you are a good worker, eventually you will be placed in a position of authority over others. When that happens, don't forget what it was like to be the new, useless employee. If you are a doctor, treat your nurses well. If you are a bank manager, treat your tellers well. Treat secretaries and custodial workers well. The same goes for your personal life. Treat your garbage man, and your postal worker, and your gardener well.

How do you do that? First, greet those who serve you by name, because there is no greater sign of respect than to learn and remember someone's name. Trust them with important work and give them the freedom to make meaningful decisions. Look for opportunities to recognize and reward them for their work. These are the people who enable you to do your job well or live a more comfortable life. If you make sure they know you appreciate not only the work they do but who they are as people, you will find yourself forever surrounded by people eager to serve you.

Embrace hard work. Embrace physical labor, the kind that takes the skin off your hands and blisters your feet. Physical exercise is of some benefit, but it is also an exercise in futility, the burning of energy for its own sake. Hard work is different. It invigorates the soul and teaches respect. Harvest some firewood with a handsaw and axe, and you will have a new appreciation for the energy it takes to heat your home. Build a wall from fieldstones, and you will have a new appreciation for the effort it takes farmers to prepare the land to produce your food. Repair your own car, and you will have a new appreciation for what it takes to get you from here to there. Hard work is all around you, a quiet teacher awaiting willing pupils. Look for opportunities to learn from her.

Embrace menial work. Scrubbing toilets is not beneath you unless you have never had need of a toilet. Cleaning a stove is not beneath you unless you have never eaten cooked food. Changing a diaper is not beneath you unless you have never had your own diaper changed. Life is full of dirty, mundane tasks. Do not scorn them; rather, embrace them as a necessity of existence and do them with pride and respect. A clean toilet or stove or diaper is something beautiful to behold, even if it stays that way only a short while. Menial tasks done well become meaningful tasks.

Do work that connects you with your world. In a working world increasingly detached from the traditional tasks of procuring shelter, food, and clothing, work that connects you to these basic tasks also connects you to your humanity. Repair and improve your own home. Mend and sew your own clothing. It doesn't matter whether you have a physical need to do these things—do them anyway. Train yourself to appreciate simple, necessary things and the work required to obtain them. Plant a garden and tend it. Harvest its bounty with gratitude, prepare your food with care, and enjoy the taste of something you have cultivated and cooked for yourself. Raise or hunt your own meat. When meat comes packaged in shrink-wrap or deep-fried in batter, it is easy to ignore that a mortal act has been carried out by someone else on your behalf. Don't attempt to absolve yourself of that act. Be willing to commit it yourself, with the honor and gravity it is due, as a grim reminder that your life comes at a cost that others must bear. And don't feel bad about it—you will be food for worms soon enough.

Maintain a healthy separation between your work and personal life. It is all too easy to let your work slowly take over your time and energy until you have none left for anything else. Do you care about your family? Your physical fitness? Your friends? Your hobby? Your community? Your home? Prove it by the way you manage your time. Work when you are at work, and live your personal life when you are not.

It is harder now than ever to maintain a clear distinction between personal life and work. Just a few decades ago, about the only people who were perpetually on call were doctors and firefighters. People understood that those whose work had life-or-death consequences had to be prepared at a moment's notice to drop whatever they were doing and report for duty. Today, the subtle expectation is that *everyone* be this accessible. Do people die if you are inaccessible for a few hours? Probably not. Don't think more highly of your work than you ought to.

If you work from home, designate specific times and physical spaces for work and specific times and physical spaces for your personal life, and then ruthlessly adhere to those boundaries. If you fail to do so, the two will seep into one another until no one ever has your full attention. Work tends to creep into your personal life more than the other way around because the obligations of work are often better defined and seem more urgent than personal obligations. At work, there is a report due on Monday by 9:00 am, and there is a boss to hold you accountable should you fail to meet that obligation. There is no such definition to the obligation to read your child a bedtime story the night before your report is due, and no boss looking over your shoulder to make sure you do it. Every opportunity to do something with your time is gone the instant that moment passes, and children soon grow too old for bedtime stories.

Be thankful. Your ancestors had to work much harder than you or I ever will. As a teacher, I was obligated to put in 30 hours a week, 220 days a year. Anything beyond that was optional, and since I was a union worker, the only thing driving me to do more than the minimum was my personal integrity. Yet my salary easily put me in the top 1% of earners in the world. My grandparents had to work three times as many hours doing harder work to provide less for their families.

Never forget that. Never forget how hard your ancestors had to work to make your life a little easier than their own. Never forget how blessed your work is. When you look upon your own accomplishments, remember that they do not belong to you alone. Your work is a debt of honor to those who have come before you and worked on your behalf.

So, I ask: *In what ways does your perspective on work need to mature?*

Educational Realities

What is education *for*? Is it to enrich your life or to prepare you for the world of work?

It always irritated a Latin-teaching friend of mine when he was asked to justify the *usefulness* of Latin. It wasn't that he couldn't make any good arguments; what irritated him was that he was asked to make any argument at all, that it was assumed that a subject had to be *useful* to be worth learning. Why learn Latin? *Because you want to know Latin!* Do you need any other reason? Must everything have economic value? Is it not acceptable to learn something entirely for its own sake?

Yes and no. It is fine to learn *some* things for their own sake, but we cannot *exclusively* learn things for their own sake or even *principally* learn things for their own sake; we must principally learn things of practical use. If I loved poetry and spent my entire day writing it but had no means of procuring food, clothing, shelter, and safety, then I wouldn't be a poet very long, would I? Animals spend nearly all their time looking after their basic necessities. We humans, by contrast, have developed such efficient methods of providing for our needs that we have created the concept of *free time*, time for doing whatever we want, like writing poetry. That is a wonderful privilege, but never forget that we must first work. Never forget that leisure comes only once our basic needs are met. If you like free time and would like to have more of it, you would be wise to pursue a career that easily provides for your basic needs. You must be tenaciously efficient with your time if you wish to do anything but work until you die.

Needs before wants. If your education fails to equip you to look after your basic needs, then it has failed you, or rather you have failed it. Take command of your education. Make sure it provides you the things you need, after which you are free to do whatever you wish with whatever time remains.

When it comes to making decisions for your future, don't worry about what others are doing—make choices that are right for you. Each of us is unique, and what is best for one is not necessarily best for another.

Not everyone is well served by going to college. There was a time when a four-year degree, any four-year degree, marked its owner as competent and primed for success, because earning a college degree was a high achievement. Not so today. Half of all humanities graduates find themselves unemployed or underemployed after college. A better job market awaits those in the sciences, but half of all freshmen who start science degrees don't finish them. Never before has a four-year degree cost more, provided less, or been a bigger risk.

Why are prospects so bleak in a land of such opportunity? First, colleges are big business. Don't let their non-profit status fool you: They want your money, and to get it they are happy to teach you whatever it is you want to learn. You're willing to pay $100,000 for a degree in Art History? We teach that. African-American Studies? We teach that, too. Sports Marketing? No problem. Colleges are factories run on the same principle as other businesses: supply and demand. If they have students lining up to study something, they will line up professors to teach it. Will they warn you ahead of time that most of those who start a particular program don't finish or that job prospects for its graduates are poor? No and no. Whether you drop out after a few years or can't find a job after college, the school you've attended will end up with tens of thousands of dollars of your money.

Did I say *your* money? I didn't really mean that. As expensive as it is, few people can afford to pay for college with their own savings. That's where a giant, enabling bureaucracy comes in to... save you? The government is just as indiscriminate as the colleges it funds, doling out loans to students pursuing Interpretive Dance just as readily as it does to those pursuing Mechanical Engineering. The government doesn't have to care whether your degree is a good investment because student loans are non-dischargeable in bankruptcy. That's right: Your student loans stay wrapped around your neck, no matter how badly things go for you, until you pay them off or die.

Loose admissions and lending practices lead to a general perception among young people that they are well served by going to college and taking on the necessary debt to do so. After all, if it weren't a good idea, why would schools admit me? Why would the government and banks lend me the money? Why would everyone from parents to politicians tell me that a college degree is essential to a successful life?

The reality is that college is a bad idea for those who are poor students or choose their majors poorly. It takes wisdom to ignore the nice people who have been filling your psyche with flattering words of affirmation since you were born: "You're talented!" "You're special!" "Follow your dreams!" "You can do anything!" These are usually lies. Most of us are not all that talented or special, or those words would cease to mean what they mean. The vacuous affirmations of well-intentioned adults lead young people by the millions to make terrible decisions for their future. Don't be one of them. Instead, have a humble, accurate view of your potential. Think critically about your dreams, and if they're bad dreams, find better ones. When people shower you with flattery, *you* must be the wisest person in your life. *You* must recognize lies for what they are, especially those you want to believe.

Fifty years ago, 50% of high-school students went to college. Now, 70% do. Colleges fifty years ago could therefore afford to admit only above-average students; now about 30% of students in college were already below-average in *high school*. How well do these below-average students fare? Well, that depends on the metrics you use. If your SAT score is below 1000 or your ACT score below 21, then you are below average by those metrics. Unless your scores are either well below or well above these averages, however, standardized test scores are not great predictors of college performance. A much better predictor is *high-school GPA*, which is based less on how smart you are and more on how responsible you are—it is the diligent, not the brilliant, who get good grades in high school. But isn't college different? Isn't being smart what matters there? Only if you are also self-disciplined. Colleges provide much less structure and support than high schools do; should it come as any surprise that the responsible also fare better there?

Only 40% of college entrants graduate with four-year degrees in four years. That number climbs to 60% if they are given six years to finish. Only 25% of part-time students graduate with four-year degrees, and only 40% of students who enroll at two-year colleges graduate at all. College is a huge risk. How good a risk is it for you? That depends on how well prepared you are to succeed once you get there. So, how well prepared are you? Be sure you answer that question honestly before you begin taking on debt.

Ah, debt. One of the best predictors of college completion is how much money a student's family has. Students from poorer families enroll in college at lower rates, and once enrolled they complete their degrees at *far* lower rates. Not only do they face greater financial hurdles; they also tend to be less academically prepared, have fewer educational role models, and receive less social support.

College admissions practices designed to help the disadvantaged often end up accomplishing the opposite. Because poor students are disproportionately Black, Hispanic, and Native American, they are often admitted to fulfill racial quotas. That may sound great for them, but it often isn't, because they generally have among the lowest academic credentials of those in their programs and are therefore among those most likely to drop out. Schools have admissions quotas; they don't have graduation quotas. Colleges even guarantee transfers to replacement students years in advance because they know a certain percentage of each incoming class, including a disproportionate number of Blacks, Hispanics, and Native Americans, will drop out. This is why it is so critical that you assess your own situation honestly; you cannot count on colleges to do it for you. Attending the most prestigious program that admits you is not necessarily in your best interest. Those in the bottom half of their incoming classes are already more than likely to drop out—imagine your odds if you begin in the bottom ten percent!

The quality of your education has much more to do with what you put into it than what your college does. When you go to a prestigious school, much of what you are paying for is the school's reputation, a reputation often earned more for its research than for its instruction. A school may have professors who have won Nobel Prizes, but how many have won Nobel Prizes for *teaching*? You must ask yourself whether you would be better served at a giant school with a big name, one of hundreds of freshmen in your introductory classes, or at a smaller, less prestigious school, with professors who know you by name and whose primary focus is instructing *you*. The name of the school on your diploma may open a few doors after you graduate, but your long-term success will depend much more on how well your education has prepared your brain for thinking and your body for doing. What matter most are the sort of person you have become and the sort of work you can do, and those depend mostly on *you*.

You may not have to work very hard in high school to get into college, but to succeed once you get there you must be prepared. Colleges often design freshman classes specifically to weed out as quickly as possible those who cannot handle the rigors of the program. Remember, before you even set foot on campus, there are students at other schools already lined up to take your place should you stumble out of the gates. Freshmen classes can be punishing, and your brain and psyche must be prepared to withstand that punishment. Preparing for college by taking cupcake classes in high school is like preparing to run a marathon by eating cupcakes. Train your mind instead to run long and hard while also taking care not to burn yourself out along the way. You don't have to run marathons to train for a marathon, but you do have to train with a purpose.

Dropping out of college is in many ways worse than not attending college at all: First is the crippling debt you stand to incur; second is the loss of time you could have spent moving in a better direction; third is the loss of heart you experience from having failed at the very first thing you set out to do as an adult. By every measure, dropping out of college is a terrible way to start your adult life. I repeat: College is a huge risk. Be sure you are prepared before you take it.

So, I ask: *How well prepared are you for the academic and financial realities of college? What would you need to do to become better prepared?*

Other Options

Have you ever thanked your neighbors for paying their taxes so you could attend school? Would you be proud to go door to door with your transcript to prove to them that their money has been well spent? One student's K-12 education typically costs taxpayers upwards of $150,000. If after receiving that education you are only capable of doing unskilled labor, taxpayers will have gotten precious little return on their investment. Has your education been worth $150,000? What have you done to ensure that it has?

The sad truth is that, unless you go through a vocational or technical program, a K-12 education provides you with few marketable skills. In earlier times, a high-school diploma, like a college diploma, was worth more than it is today because it was harder to obtain. Graduation from high school was once an exceptional achievement. In 1910, the U.S. high-school graduation rate was about 10%. That rate rose steadily over ensuing decades as U.S. public schools became the envy of the world, reaching 75% during the 1960s, the zenith of U.S. scientific, engineering, and manufacturing dominance. Over the three decades that followed, the rate declined slightly.

Then came the age of highly publicized high-school rankings. Imagine yourself a school administrator pressured to improve your school's standing. How would you do it? By demanding higher achievement? That would require both better teaching from your unionized labor force and more enthusiastic participation from your most apathetic students. But wait—there would be an easier way. Simply *lower academic standards*: Inflate grades and reduce graduation requirements, and more students would graduate. Not only would your school's standing rise, but your students and their parents, rather than complain that their education has been diminished, would *thank* you! This is exactly what school administrators have done.

Since 1998, high-school graduation rates have risen from 70% to 85%, the highest they have ever been, while American students are statistically no more capable than before.

The problem is that if all you have to do to graduate is drool on your desk for four years, then not only *your* diploma but *every* diploma is no better than a certificate of attendance. Prospective employers are no fools; they know this. A high-school diploma no longer means almost anything in the workplace. It is only of consequence if you *don't* have one, because why would an employer want to hire someone unable or unwilling to complete something as easy as *high school*?

The problem, though, goes deeper than our schools. Prospects in our workforce for the poorly educated have dwindled as well. As the American standard of living increased in the middle of the last century, American workers began demanding higher pay, prompting manufacturers to mechanize and move their operations overseas. Once the most prolific exporter in the world, America became a net importer about fifty years ago, and it hasn't looked back. What does that mean for you? Most of the unskilled jobs once done by your grandparents and great-grandparents are now done by foreigners and machines; they are no longer options for you.

All this is to say that a high-school diploma is no longer good enough. You need to distinguish yourself with more than that, with better than that. As we've established, though, a college education is expensive and of dubious value. So, what should you do? Don't worry. You're one of the most privileged people ever to walk the face of the earth. You have options.

Scholarly information used to reside in musty libraries and was curated by a small community of people who commanded handsome sums to teach it to you. A good education was the luxury of the wealthy. But now! Now the click of a button transports a boy or girl from the ghetto to worlds of knowledge they couldn't hope to consume in a thousand lifetimes. Have you ever found yourself wondering, "Why should I pay tens of thousands of dollars a year to learn in pretentious old buildings what I could learn while sitting in my living room, or on the subway, or on the beach in Acapulco?" You should. It is exactly the right question to ask.

Things are changing. There are already schools and professional cooperatives that offer online courses at a fraction of what traditional colleges charge and will teach you everything you need to know to succeed in the working world. Some are even free! The potential is so obvious that even traditional colleges, teetering like dinosaurs on a tightrope, have lumbered into the marketplace, attempting to parlay their fancy names into lucrative profits. As the competition gets fiercer, however—and it will—schools that don't get leaner will have their fat flesh consumed until there is little left. Education simply no longer needs to cost as much as it does, and people are beginning to realize it. Change, however, comes slowly, and today's reality is today's reality. Your options may cost more than they should, but at least you have options.

With remote learning there are, of course, sacrifices. There are always sacrifices. Remote learning strips away the rich cultural tapestry of college life and demands greater independence on the part of the learner. If that worries you, remember that the most important factor in determining the value of your education is *you*, and the clearest mark of your maturity as a learner is your ability to teach yourself. Whatever you choose to study and however you choose to study it, *you* must ultimately take upon *yourself* the responsibility for learning it. The goal of education, after all, is to become an independent learner and thinker. Are you up to that task? If not, don't expect a college to magically make you capable of it.

Not all fields of study translate equally well to remote learning. Some types of education will always remain in-person and expensive, and rightly so. You may be able to get a quality education in the liberal arts from your living room, because it mostly requires reading good books and having smart people to discuss them with, but you cannot become a surgeon that way, or an electrical engineer, or a carpenter, or an auto-body repair technician. Disciplines that require the development of specialized skills will always require extensive in-person training to acquire them.

Even so, technical schools and professional licensure programs tend to be less expensive than traditional colleges and provide excellent long-term earning potential. If you are too young to have had your plumbing repaired, or car fixed, or heating system replaced, or bathroom renovated, ask an adult what the people who do these things charge for their services—it may astound you. How about getting your teeth cleaned, or a medical scan, or physical therapy? Same thing. The people who perform these services are compensated handsomely because they are not *un*skilled but *skilled* workers, and consumers are willing to pay good money for skill. As long as people own houses, drive cars, and need medical care, skilled people will always be in demand, and if they treat their customers well and put in an honest day's work, they will be able to work on their own terms, perhaps even as their own bosses.

The military is another excellent option for the right people. In many countries, young men are conscripted into military service as a rite of passage into adulthood. In the U.S., except under extreme circumstances, young men have the luxury of choosing for themselves whether to enlist. The military life is hard; it is not for everyone. For that reason, there is a low supply and a high demand for new recruits, and wherever there is a low supply and a high demand, there are incentives. The military helps you pay for college and trains you in skills that often translate well to the private sector. It compensates you for rising through the ranks, doing active duty, and doing hazardous duty. It also allows you to retire with a full pension after just *twenty years* of service.

The sacrifices? First, you are not your own; you are owned. You are a tool in the hands of the powerful. You must go where you are ordered to go and do what you are ordered to do. You are shuttled from base to base and must live with the constant threat of being sent far away and into harm's way. You must be willing to maim or kill or be maimed or killed on command. You must adopt a mindset that enables you to thrive in combat situations but alienates you from civilian life. Psychological problems and divorce rates in the military are among the highest in any line of work.

If the military life aligns well with your calling, however, it can be both meaningful and lucrative. I recall catching up with a cousin of mine twelve years after he had enlisted in the Air Force. He was a dog-handler in a bomb patrol unit, someone who risked his life to keep others safe. He was also young and single and spent most of his time on active duty. So, I asked, what did he do with his paychecks?

He replied, "I invest them: IRAs, mutual funds, that sort of thing." "Really," I said, "and how much is your portfolio worth?" He said, "Well, I haven't looked at it recently, but probably somewhere around a million dollars." A million dollars! Here I was with a master's degree and no savings to speak of, working for a salary that barely paid the mortgage on my first home, and my cousin who had never gone to college had a million dollars in retirement savings by the age of thirty! Eight years later he would retire with a full pension. He is now in his forties and has begun a second career, gotten married, and started a family.

So, I ask: *How well does your plan for your future align with your identity and vision? What other options do you need to explore?*

The Riskiest Option

And if you still don't know what to do with your first steps into adulthood? Don't go to college just to have something to do. We've already reviewed the dropout statistics. How well do you think college goes for those who have no idea why they're there?

Instead, consider a gamble: a gap year. A gap year is an immense risk, because once out of the academic world it can be hard to get back into it. To mitigate that risk, you may be wise to apply to schools beforehand and then defer your admission. That way, if your gap year doesn't help you figure things out, you have something to come back to. A well-planned gap year, though, *should* help you figure things out. It could change your entire perspective on the world. But how? What could you do in a year that could be that meaningful?

Travel. Just a few hundred years ago, you would have had to spend a life's savings, take months or even years of time, and risk great harm to travel to the other side of the world. A few hundred years before that, no one had ever even done it. Today, you can traverse the globe in a day at modest cost and minimal risk. Why wouldn't you do that as often as you possibly could?

If you try this option, don't just go as a tourist to sight-see. Take time to immerse yourself in a new culture and language, working and living as the natives do. Push yourself beyond what is comfortable and experience firsthand how the poor of this world live. Do this, and you will return home with all sorts of perspective and focus, wise beyond your years and your peers—a completely different person. Or, perhaps you may find a new home altogether and never return. That's the beauty of it—you never know.

When I was thirteen, I spent a year in my mother's native Colombia, a gap year of sorts (I skipped the eighth grade—don't tell anyone). It was one of the most difficult years of my life, but it was also one of the most memorable. It opened my eyes to a world I never knew existed and changed the way I saw everything, including myself.

You are never as free to travel as you are when you are young. Do it as often as you have the opportunity.

Get a crappy job. I'm sorry, what I mean is, get the best job you can with a high-school diploma. In all likelihood, that will be a crappy job. Completely sever financial ties with your parents. Find the best housing you can afford, pay for your own food, medical care, and utilities, and arrange for your own transportation. Try that for one year and see what it does for your motivation and focus.

I once had a student who, while gifted, had little enthusiasm for high school and didn't pursue higher education after he graduated. A year later he came back to visit. I asked him what he was up to, and he said, "Working at the waffle shop." I asked him if he had any other plans, and he said, "Yeah, I'm enrolled next semester at a tech school to study heavy equipment." It was a good choice for him, a career that would challenge his mind and compensate him well for meaningful work. But why, I asked, had he changed his mind? He said, "Because working at the waffle shop sucks." He had gotten the best job he could find out of high school, and it hadn't taken him long to realize that he didn't want to make a career out of the best job he could find out of high school. Fortunately for him, he got the perspective he needed with enough time and freedom to do something about it before it was too late.

This, by the way, is one of the best reasons to work a crappy job *before* you finish high school: The sooner you figure out what you don't want to do, the sooner you'll be able to figure out what you do want to do and the better positioned you'll be to do something about it.

Serve others. Find a mission agency—religious, secular, or government-affiliated—that trains and sends young people to work with the needy, and give a year or two of your life to its work. Young people represent the most powerful force in the world, the best investment a society can make and its entire hope for the future. You are capable of great things—go do them! Put your physical and mental faculties to work for the good of others. Not only would it leave you with perspective borne from first-hand experience; it would also enable you to approach the rest of your life with the confidence that comes from already having done something meaningful with it.

If you take the risk of a gap, do it on a strict time frame and continue to plan for what comes next. Remember, it is all too easy once you have left the academic world never to return to it, and to succeed you must acquire more knowledge and skills than you can get in high school. Don't get lazy and stupid. A gap year should help prepare you for adulthood, not prolong your adolescence. These are the first steps you get to take on your own. Take them wisely.

So, I ask: *How will your first steps into adulthood prepare you for the rest of your life?*

The Slavery of Your Choosing

You may think that when you become an adult you will be free to do whatever you want to do. It simply doesn't work that way. The older you get, the more limited your choices become. To this point in your life, someone else has provided most of the hard things for you: food, clothing, shelter, education. Once you're out in the world, obtaining these things begins to crowd out your opportunities to do other things. When you come back home at the end of a long day of work, it can be hard to motivate yourself to do anything but sit down. When you get married, your freedom shrinks more. When you buy a house, it shrinks more. When you have children, it shrinks more. The older you get, the less and less free you are to do what you want to do.

That's not necessarily a bad thing. Your identity is ultimately defined not by what you liberate yourself from but by what you bind yourself to. Who are you? You are a seeker of whatever you seek. But why do you seek what you seek? That you might bind yourself to it. We are all in search of a master, and who and what that master is defines who and what we are. You will be a slave to someone or something, that much is certain. Your choice is to whom and what you would be enslaved, and your opportunity to make that choice for yourself dwindles with each passing day. An urgent decision is upon you, *right now*. To whom and what would you be enslaved? *That* is where your freedom lies, while you have it. *That* is where your choices lie, while you have them. Make them soon, and make them well, and you will live a life of happy enslavement to the binds of your choosing. Slave work can be immensely gratifying if you have the right master.

Beware of whom you owe and how much, because to owe is to have a master. Whether you marry, pledge yourself in service to a cause, partner with a friend on a business venture, accept a favor, buy on credit, or commit yourself to care for someone in need, you are choosing a master. I have a friend who in his forties felt called to become a missionary to one of the neediest countries in the world. The organization he had served full-time for two decades as a pastor, however, refused to send him because he and his wife still had tens of thousands of dollars in unpaid college debt. Can you imagine being told you're too poor to become a *missionary*? He had sought to dedicate his life to God, yet there he was, twenty years into a life of service, still bound to another master. Eventually, he found an organization that would accept him with his debt, but how would he pay it off while living as a missionary? His *children* were about to go off to college, and he still had his *own* college debt to worry about! As a young person starting out with little to call your own, debt can be an alluring master, but beware, because it can keep you in its grips in perpetuity and hinder you from obeying the higher calls of better masters.

Consider two college freshmen, one pursuing Sociology and the other Dentistry. The first student's education will cost $100,000 and take him four years to complete, the second student's $200,000 and take her eight years. The problem for the first student is, once he graduates, what is he qualified to *do*? A college friend of mine studying Sociology nervously joked as we approached graduation, "When I go into a job interview and they ask me what I can do, what am I supposed to say, that I can *understand people*?" He had spent four years obtaining an expensive education in soft skills, and he knew it. Likely, his first job would be as a counselor or social worker making $35,000 per year. How long would it take to pay off his college loans at that salary? How long before he could own a house or begin saving for his own children's education? At that salary, a hundred thousand dollars of debt might feel like a million.

Compare that with the situation of our burgeoning dentist. She stands to incur twice as much debt, but she would likely start her career making $100,000 per year, giving her a clear path to paying it off quickly. Much better, right? *Maybe*. What if her education gets derailed? A lot can happen in eight years. If she ends up stopping short with, say, a four-year degree in Biology, what will become of her larger goals? Will she still be able to pay off her debt quickly? Will her new career and life prospects still please her?

Let's imagine another angle on this second scenario. What if our aspiring dentist also dreams of one day becoming a stay-at-home mother? How much does one aspiration stand to disrupt the other? If she gets $200,000 in debt and then marries at age twenty-seven, she may have to put off becoming a mother another five to ten years just to pay off her debt. By the time she does that, she may be nearing the end of her childbearing years and be faced with giving up an established practice to have children. Sacrifices are always made.

More women face this type of conundrum than you may imagine, and the hypothetical example I gave was of a woman who was *extremely successful*. What would it look like had this woman instead become a social worker? The contented career mom is atypical. Most working mothers report that they wish they could stay home full-time with their children. If you wish one day to become a stay-at-home mother, you must plan your career timeline especially carefully and make certain you can pay off your debt quickly. Otherwise, you may become a slave to your debt, trudging off to work every day while you leave your children in childcare not because you feel called to but because you are forced to. It is all too easy to enslave yourself to the wrong master.

That said, it is still important for women who wish to be stay-at-home mothers to be capable of financial independence should things not work out the way they hope. One of the primary reasons women get into and stay in bad relationships is financial. It is all too easy to enslave yourself to the wrong master.

Don't like to think of yourself as a slave-in-training? Fine. Consider an alternative analogy: Imagine you have fifty days ahead of you, and you're given a choice: Do whatever you want to do for eight days and then have others tell you what to do for the next forty-two, or work really hard for eight days and then do whatever you want to do for the next forty-two. Easy choice, right? Well, that's precisely the choice before you, only what faces you is not fifty *days* but fifty *years*. Spend the first eight years (roughly the time needed for high school and some form of higher education) doing whatever you want to do and the next forty-two having others tell you what to do, or work really hard for those eight years and spend the next forty-two doing whatever you want to do.

This analogy is not my own but that of a fellow teacher, a licensed contractor who owns a construction business on the side. He spent eight years working really hard acquiring skills and certifications, and now he has forty-two years to do whatever he wants to do. Whenever he's unsatisfied with what he's doing, he quits his job and starts something new. What gives him that freedom? The hard work he has put into developing himself coupled with the self-confidence that comes from having taken good risks along the way.

Whether you see your education as preparation for freedom or slavery is merely a matter of perspective; the two ideas are really one and the same. My teacher/contractor friend has a great many responsibilities, things he has to do. Owning a business and teaching full-time speak for most of his hours, and his wife and children take up what's left. Yet, even if his whole week's time is spoken for before he wakes up Monday morning, he wakes up happy to have his hours spoken for in this way. He freely enjoys the slavery of his choosing.

So, I ask: *What would you need to do with what remains of your eight years to prepare you for the life you desire for the next forty-two? To whom and what would you be enslaved?*

A Time for Action

Truth is truth, a respecter of no one, and a lie is a lie, no matter how craftily it is told. I have aimed to speak the truth throughout this book, so I can say with a clear conscience that I have not lied to you. But the truth is elusive, and it doesn't take a lie to miss it; one need only be wrong. I am sure I am wrong about some of the things I've written—it's not as if I have everything figured out myself—but I won't apologize. I told you from the beginning to question everything I had to say, to expose it to the most rigorous testing you could muster. Have you? Even if you have, you must recognize that you, too, could be wrong, and may even have reason to lie to yourself. None of us, after all, are very reliable judges of truth and falsehood. The world, however, is. Regardless of what we *believe* to be true, the world will eventually teach us what *is* true, if it doesn't kill us first. It may be a cruel teacher, but it is reliable.

And it is slow.

There are a great many things you do not know, and yet even when you do not know, you are often required to act as if you do. You may not know how best to spend your money at the grocery store, but you still have to eat, so you do the best you can in spite of your ignorance. There is no shame in doing that. Acting in spite of our ignorance is what we all do every minute of every day in a thousand ways. You may not know for sure whether God exists, or what makes the sky blue, or what someone you love is thinking, or why your car is making that funny sound, or even who you are, but you must act in spite of your ignorance. Time is a relentless slavedriver, and so you must act and do your best. Or not do your best. Or even choose evil over good. But you don't have the option not to act at all. Not acting is itself an action, and not a particularly productive one. Even as you sit idly by, the world moves on and your heart beats on, and it will not beat forever.

Now is the time for action, for transitioning from figuring out what needs to be done to actually doing it. What can you do *right now*? Life is a series of actions and reflections. I have encouraged you to do a lot of reflection, but reflection can become an excuse for inaction, a justification for indolence. Don't be lazy. Act. Now.

Even as you act, remember that you act in ignorance. Don't get so lost in action that you forget to take time to ponder life's essential questions. Keep them ever before you. This book opened with one of these questions: *Why bother doing anything?* How did you answer that question when you first pondered it? How would you answer it now? Perhaps your original answer already feels foreign to you, as if those thoughts weren't your thoughts at all but belonged to some other person entirely, some younger, naiver person who lived long ago. And perhaps they are. Perhaps you are no longer the same person you were. Perhaps a transformation has begun in you. That transformation doesn't have to end. Your life can become a continual series of deaths and rebirths if you continue to ask life's big questions, listen for its call, and aim well. Who knows where you may end up, what sort of a person you may become? Nothing is certain in this adventure of life, but what an adventure it is!

I don't know how things will turn out for you. Your life will likely be some combination of blessings and hardships, joy and pain, as long as it lasts. Life is one giant, beautiful risk. It makes you no guarantees, so I make you no guarantees.

But I do have hope.

I consider it my great privilege that you have allowed me to cast these few seeds before you, my great honor that you have taken the time to sift through them. My hope is that you have found the process difficult, that having gone through it makes everything else you go through in life a little easier. My hope is that you grab hold of life with conviction, that you embrace its chaos with a determined and sober mind, with a firm knowledge of who you are and why you do what you do. My hope is that, when you come to the end of your life, you will be able to say you have lived it well.

I also have faith. I not only *hope* you to be capable of greatness but *know* you to be capable of it. But how? How could I possibly know that when I don't even know you? Because I've known that about every student I've ever taught, even before meeting them. Every fall, in the quiet of an empty classroom, I would read over a list of names with the same knowledge of the strangers on that list that I have of you. I knew that they all, like you, were capable of greatness.

Then I would meet them. I would come face-to-face with their talents and inadequacies, their enthusiasm and apathy, the obstacles placed before them by life and those they'd placed before themselves. But those things never shook my faith. When my students left my class, whether they had earned an 'A' or an 'F', had dropped out of school or were bound for the Ivy League, were an Eagle Scout or a drug addict, my faith never wavered. We all take different paths through life, some straight, some crooked, some that meander all over the place. Just because my students were not yet what they could become did not mean they would never become it.

My faith is not a blind faith. I've seen too many of the unlikeliest succeed for me to doubt the rest. I've had a student with a troubled personal life show complete apathy for my class and fail it, only to take command of her life over the summer, sign up for my class again the following fall, and ace it. I've had an otherwise unremarkable Chinese student begin the school year so deficient in English that he had to translate everything he read or wrote one word at a time, only to will himself from the bottom to the top of my advanced class in *four months*. I've had a student scuffle through my class with a drug problem, only to turn her life around so dramatically that she eventually became a youth leader and now mentors my own children. These are just a few of the stories I know. How many do I not know? I may never know. But I know enough never to lose hope or faith in a single person. Every time I see a boy squandering his potential, every time I see a girl making a mess of her life, I remind myself, "They are not yet what they shall become." Likewise, you are not yet what you shall become. Don't let the *not yet* deter you from the *could be*. Don't despair in your present situation or most recent failure. You are not what you shall become! Be patient with yourself. Only after a season of your life has passed will you be able to fully appreciate what it has done for you. When your best efforts are met with a punch to the face, wipe the blood from your mouth, force a smile, and better your best efforts. When you act so shamefully you can't stand to look at yourself in the mirror the following morning, splash some cold water on your face, resolve to make whatever amends you must, and begin redeeming yesterday today.

My faith is not a naive faith. Even while I knew that every one of my students *could* be great, I also knew that not every one of them *would* be. I could not make them attain greatness; I could only encourage them in the pursuit of it. I could not overcome their obstacles for them; I could only show them how they might do it for themselves. I know that not every person who reads this will succeed, not because they *can't* but because they *won't*, and yet even when they *don't* I remain steadfast in my faith that they *can*. So it is with my faith in you. I have no way of knowing whether you *will* succeed; I only know that you *can*.

My faith is not a vacuous faith. After all, it could simply be that those who would have succeeded anyway will succeed regardless, and that those who wouldn't have won't. But my faith is not a meaningless faith in those who would have succeeded anyway, nor is it a generic faith in humanity as a whole. My faith is specific and concrete. I do not simply believe that *some* can succeed—I believe that *you* can.

My faith is not a conditional faith. I believe in you no matter how lazy you are, or unskilled, or weak, or damaged, or immature, or immoral. I will continue to believe in you no matter what a mess you make of your life or how badly you waste your potential. My faith remains every moment you live, because as long as you have breath in your lungs, your story is not finished. As long as you live, you have the opportunity to redeem every moment of your life, to turn every evil into a good.

How can I prove my faith to you? The same way I proved it to my students; the same way a few teachers proved it to me when I was a lost young man: by expecting you to be great. I don't just *hope* you will be great. I don't just have faith that you *can* be great. I fully *expect* you to be great.

But my hope, my faith, and my expectation are irrelevant—they are beside the point. There is no tyranny here. There is always a choice, and that choice is yours. That hope must be yours. That faith must be yours. That expectation must be yours.

So, go! Be great! Stop reading a book about being great and go be great!

Or don't. It's up to you.

So, I ask: *What is your hope? What is your faith? What is your expectation?*

The Talk is over.

Now is the time for action.
But what action should you take?

Visit
www.shawndaviswriting.com
for your free copy of
A Guide to Action.

Or don't. It's up to you.

www.ingramcontent.com/pod-product-compliance
Lightning Source LLC
Chambersburg PA
CBHW072013040426
42447CB00009B/1616